Hunter, Faith and the Ancestors

AN ADOPTION STORY
OF CHANGE AND BELONGING

By Serena Patterson, Ph. D.

With Parent Chapters By Dr. Serena Patterson, Ph. D.
and Monika Grünberg, Clinical Counsellor
Illustrated by Claire Kujunzic

Co-authored by Monika Grünberg

Illustrations by Claire Kujunzic

ISBN

978-1-4602-2442-7 (Hardcover)

978-1-4602-2443-4 (Paperback)

978-1-4602-2444-1 (eBook)

Produced by:

FriesenPress

Suite 300 – 852 Fort Street

Victoria, BC, Canada V8W 1H8

www.friesenpress.com

Distributed to the trade by The Ingram Book Company

Table of Contents

Faith and Hunter: The Parent Chapters

Dedication

To all my children, by birth and by choice, And to the
animals, too, who have taught us all so much about love.

Chapter 1: The Little People

Faith Green was mad. She was furious. She was so mad she could explode. But she wouldn't explode. No, she would get even.

She took a bouncy ball from the bowl of them she kept on her dresser and threw it against the wall with all her might. The ball bounced against the floor, the ceiling, the chest of dress-up clothes and the ceiling again. Pow, pow, pow, until it came to rest, buried in her pile of stuffies. Steaming, Faith climbed onto her dresser with a handful of the bouncy missiles. "What's the matter?" Helen and Toni kept asking. "What's wrong? How can we fix it?" Over and over, like they expected her to give an answer. It was a trick; they knew good and well that everything was wrong.

Take this afternoon for instance. After a perfectly satisfactory day at school, Faith had arrived "home" at three o'clock. But where was Helen? Upstairs, working on something on her computer. No "hello, Faith", no cookies and milk. "Just a minute, honey!" she said, when Faith appeared at her study door. And when Faith came in to stand at her shoulder, Helen closed what she was looking at, turned with a grumpy look and sighed, "Those are your outdoor shoes, Faith. Where are your slippers?" Mothers were supposed to greet you after school with cookies and a smile, weren't they? Helen told other people that she was Faith's mother, but she was pretending.

Then Faith wanted to go up the street to where the boys played on bicycles and skateboards. "No, not yet," said Helen, knowing full well that everyone else would be gathering already. "You need to gather your clothes for washing, do your reading, and practice for your piano lesson. Oh, and the dishwasher needs cleaning out."

What did Helen think she was? A slave? A servant?

Then there was the snack. "You can have an apple, or toast." Great. The same every day—an apple or toast. Didn't she know that kids are supposed to eat a variety of foods? What instruction manual did Helen read on kids, for heaven's sake? One published in 1958?

No computer until the chores are done. No playing outside until after snack. No running in the house. And now, just because Roscoe yipped, just once, no dog in the bedroom. Well, not with the door closed. And having Roscoe in her room with the door open didn't work—Roscoe would leave. That's why Faith needed the cup full of kibbles that she kept on her dresser. But of course, those were illegal, too.

Roscoe, her one friend. Roscoe with the kind eyes, the brown silky fur. Roscoe who would chase a ball any time, any where, and bring it back again and again. Roscoe who could jump so high, with all four feet at once, who never, ever ran out of energy to play before Faith did, and who didn't tell on her, especially when she snuck kibbles into her bedroom to feed him by hand. Roscoe was the one reason why Faith had agreed to come to the Green's. Well, that and the fact that nobody gave her any other choices.

She had been perfectly happy with the Martins—she loved her room, her toys, and her foster parents, George and Ruby. George liked to show her things in his shop, and Ruby made her macaroni and cheese exactly the way she liked it. Good old Kraft Dinner, perfect the way it was, without adding any hot dogs or peas, the way Helen and Toni did.

But George and Ruby were getting too old, they said, for kids. And then they moved to an apartment where kids weren't even allowed! Hunter said that the Greens were pretty nice, and that he and Faith had to understand the situation. After all, Ruby would be almost eighty before Faith graduated from high school, and what seventy-five-year-old wants two teenagers? Faith had to admit that seventy-five was pretty old; older than she could ever imagine becoming. But Hunter was only eleven now, and Faith was eight, so why not wait until she was a teenager? Weren't they still children? But now, her room was gone and her toys were "outgrown" and some of them were given away, and she had to put up with Helen and Toni doing everything wrong and the only thing right was Roscoe.

Now, to top it all off, she was stuck in her room just because she wouldn't answer Helen's stupid questions and because she closed the door a little bit too hard. She couldn't even go up the street to escape.

Faith descended from the dresser-top and opened the door a little, so Roscoe could come in. She made a nest on the floor with her blankets for the two of them. Roscoe snuggled in and put his head on her knee. He really was a great dog, and Faith would be a dog, too, if she had the choice. Just wag, bark, play, and sleep. Okay, eating kibble every day might be kind of gross. But at least you wouldn't have to talk when you didn't want to.

"Roscoe, you are so lucky," Faith said, stroking his silky ears and feeding him one kibble after another. "But wouldn't you like to go to school? Yes, you would. It's fun at school, and everybody likes me. Almost. It's not boring like here."

"Boring. Now that's a word I don't remember saying much in my life," said a voice.

"Roscoe?" asked Faith, confused.

"Nope, just me," said the voice coming from her desktop. And there, from behind the lamp, strode a tiny old woman, in a pink stretchy pantsuit like something on That 70's Show, with white, no, blue hair.

"What the ..." said Faith. Then she shook her head. "Who are you?"

"I don't guess you'd remember me, since you were just a baby when I passed. But Hunter does. I'm your Nana. Nana Rose."

"No," said Faith. "You are Mr. Binker."

"Mr. Binker?"

"Yes, Mr. Binker. My imaginary friend. You live in my finger. I saw it in a Muppet movie."

"Well, Missy, I'm no 'Mr.', I don't live in your finger, I've never been in a movie in my life, or my after-life, either, and I don't know who this Binker fellow is. But I am your Nana Rose. I'd have appeared full size, but I figured this was safer; I'd hate you to think somebody had broken into your bedroom. You'd probably have called the police on me."

"Well, yes. Maybe I still will."

"And say what? A tiny old woman is in your bedroom? No, they won't believe you. You might as well get used to it—you have ancestors, Missy. You need our help, and we've come to give it." And with that, Nana Rose was joined by three other tiny, slightly transparent people. There was a bald-headed fat man with a stained but friendly smile and a pipe in his front shirt pocket; a thin, muscular fellow in a yellow raincoat and hat, and a powerful-looking woman in very old-fashioned dress, hands on her hips, with red curls and a turned up nose who looked, despite her weird clothes, quite a bit like Toni. There they stood, or sat, as some stools began to take shape, and a small pot-bellied stove. The bald fat man took out his pipe and lit it. Didn't he read the warnings on tobacco? Faith could see the smoke, but there was no smell at all. Were they there? Or was she going crazy?

Roscoe got up, sniffed the people curiously, then settled back down. Evidently their lack of smell or substance didn't bother him. "That's funny," said Faith. "I thought dogs were supposed to be afraid of ghosts."

"Humph," said the wiry one, shedding his rain gear to reveal arms with muscles like ropes and a waffle-weave pullover. "Shows what you know. Roscoe's family. He's been around a few times before—right, feller?" Roscoe wagged his tail. "So, what's this revenge you're planning?"

Chapter 2: Hunter and Faith

Hunter could tell the minute he entered the house that Faith was having another meltdown. The air was thick. Helen, or "Mum", as he was trying to remember to call her, was standing at the bottom of the stairs, looking up toward an empty landing and closed bedroom doors. But the sound of bouncy balls was unmistakable. Faith had stormed off, and was throwing the balls around her bedroom. Another evening in Paradise, he thought, as he headed upstairs to read.

The problem with Faith, he thought, was that she took it too seriously. Faith was so young when they were taken into foster care and placed with the Martins. She knew that they had another mother before that, but it wasn't real to her. Ruby was like Faith's mum, and George was like her dad, and Faith didn't remember when things were different. She had come to believe that the Martin's house would be their home forever. Hunter had always known better.

Foster care wasn't supposed to be permanent. Foster children might be almost one of the family, but it was the "almost" that mattered. For foster children, family was one of those things that you couldn't take too seriously, because if you thought it was serious then you'd get disappointed for sure.

Hunter knew that life was different for him and Faith. Regular kids had "babysitters", not "respite workers." Regular kids went on vacation with their regular parents; foster kids went to "respite homes" while their foster parents went on vacations to get some "time alone." Regular kids had their pictures on the wall, not with twenty or more other kids who had lived there before, but just by themselves, or with their real sisters or brothers. There were baby pictures, and sometimes even baby shoes saved for regular kids. Nobody wanted to fondly remember the baby-hoods of foster kids.

Hunter liked the Martins, and knew how lucky they had been to live there for five whole years—from grade one all the way to grade six. Most foster kids moved a lot more. Several had come and gone from the Martins' house in the time that he and Faith had lived there. At the Martins, there was no hitting, no drinking alcohol, and the food was good. They got to watch TV and play video games, but only shows and games that were not violent. The Martin house made him feel quieter inside than anywhere else in the whole world. But forever? No, he had never counted on forever.

Ruby and George Martin were old people. Fostering, they said, was their job, like teaching or pumping gas or fixing the plumbing. They did it for a living. When they finally took Faith and Hunter on a vacation, and introduced them to their own grown-up children, Hunter knew that this was very special treatment. They wanted to create memories, Ruby had said. Memories to look back upon when Faith and Hunter lived somewhere else. Memories for after Ruby and George retired from fostering.

What it all went to show, Hunter thought, was that you couldn't get attached to people, or places. A person should always have a "Plan B."

The Greens, like the Martins, were okay people. They didn't hit, drink alcohol, or fight much. They bickered, but he had yet to see either of them get really angry. It would do for Hunter until he turned sixteen.

At sixteen, he would get a job, and get an apartment. Then, Hunter would find his dad, and it would be like old times. That was Hunter's Plan B.

Even though he had only been four years old, Hunter remembered living with his dad like it was yesterday. He made blanket forts and got to sleep in them every night if he wanted to. He got to eat what he wanted. He played video games and he didn't have to take care of Faith, because he hadn't even met her yet. Then one day his dad dropped him off at his grandmother's house and didn't come back. A few days later, Hunter's mum Roxanne came and picked him up, and, presto! There was Faith sitting in a car seat, already a crawling, crying, diaper-messing machine with an attitude.

Living with Roxanne and Faith lasted three years, but they sure covered a lot of territory. They lived in six houses, and Hunter went to three schools by the time he finished kindergarten. Faith's dad, Roger, was there sometimes, and so were lots of other people. Sometimes it was like a party, with music and food. Roxanne could cook really well, and he still missed her hamburgers and fried potatoes, bacon and eggs. But at other times, she had been missing or passed out, and he had to see what he could find in the kitchen; bread, bologna, cold cereal or Kraft Dinner straight from the box.

Then Faith would cry for no reason, and follow him everywhere. Once, the police came to arrest Roxanne, and she fought and screamed bad words at Roger. On the day the police took the children to foster care, Roxanne wasn't there and Roger was asleep on the couch. Hunter had thought she worked, but that was when he was little. Now, he thought differently. She had been taking drugs, or looking for drugs, or earning money to buy drugs. Roxanne could be fun and she could be nice, but drugs were ruining her life, so the children had to go live with the Martins in foster care.

But somewhere out there, Hunter figured his dad still loved him and might come back.

Hunter hadn't seen his dad since he was seven, when he picked him up from the Martins and they played video games at the arcade. It had been so great! He got to shoot animals, drive, box, and fly a plane, all in that one afternoon. Then they ate pizza and French fries, because

Hunter couldn't decide which he wanted. They drank Root Beer, and afterward, they went for ice cream.

Hunter's dad Gary was almost seven feet tall, and drove big trucks. Roxanne used to tell Hunter stories about how dangerous his father's job was, driving in all conditions and on mountain roads. Sometimes, he even went off the road and the rig tipped over. But he must have been a very good driver, because he always survived. That's what Roxanne said, anyway. Hunter thought that maybe God was taking care of his dad so that when he got older, they could be together.

A truck driver like Gary couldn't be expected to raise a little kid. He would be gone all the time, and when he was home, he'd have to sleep or relax. Also, he probably didn't know anything about raising little kids, and maybe he was afraid he'd mess it up if he tried. And then there was Faith, who wasn't even Gary's kid, and Gary probably thought she was still in diapers. Somehow, Faith had become Hunter's job to look after, though it didn't seem fair sometimes.

When he turned sixteen, Hunter would knock on Gary's door, and say something like, "Hi, Dad!". Then Gary would see that Hunter was grown up, and didn't need to be taken care of anymore. Faith would be thirteen and could look after herself. Hunter could cook, and take care of the house, and his dad would be proud of him.

Yes, it helped to have a Plan B. Ruby had a saying, "this too shall pass." She used it to cheer herself up when she didn't like what was going on right then in her life. Hunter hadn't understood it when he was Faith's age, but now he did. It meant, "don't get too comfortable, and don't get too freaked out. Everything will change. Just wait it out." Hunter knew how to blend in, bide his time and not cause a problem. Ruby's philosophy had become his own, and it was working.

The sound of bouncy balls brought Hunter's thoughts back to Faith. He sincerely hoped that her temper did not cause them to be moved from the Greens' before he turned sixteen. They could be annoying, and they didn't believe in TV or video games. But Hunter liked the dog, and now that he was getting used to it, the food was pretty good. There was lots of it, anyway; Toni liked to feed him like there was no tomorrow. Pancakes, spaghetti, grilled cheese sandwiches, oatmeal with apples and yogurt. Even the bread was homemade. Things could certainly be worse. Once the social worker took you to McDonalds for a "talk", you could find yourself anywhere.

"Faith!" he called out as he passed her room in the hallway, "please stop doing that. You're ruining our chances of going swimming tomorrow." Strangely, there was no answer—not so much as a bouncy ball thrown at the door. She'd suddenly gone quiet. Hunter shrugged, and vowed to check in after he scouted out the situation downstairs. He ditched his backpack in his room and headed back to the kitchen to see what there was for a snack, and what he could find out from Helen.

Chapter 3: Hunter Checks In

When Hunter entered Faith's room, she put her finger over her lips to motion him to be quiet. Then she pointed to her dresser-top, where four people, each about ten inches tall, stood or sat. A fat, bald man sat in the kind of easy chair with wings on the sides, and he removed his pipe to smile in a friendly manner between puffs. A rangy-looking fellow in rain gear had pulled up a stool and was lighting up a pipe of his own. Nana Rose nodded to Hunter as though she'd been expecting him, and a woman in very old-fashioned clothes looked him up and down before giving a slight smile of approval. Hunter was impressed.

"Cool! How'd you do that?" he asked Faith. "Is it a projector or something?"

"I didn't do it! I can't find a projector, and they answer questions and stuff so I don't think they are holograms. They say they're ancestors, like ghosts. And I'm starting to believe them!"

Hunter walked around the three exposed sides of the dresser, staring. Finally, the guy in the raincoat spoke out. "Enough of this! What do ya think yer seein'? We're yer ancestors; we didn't come here to be gawked at like some three-eyed fish. We've got stuff to talk about. The sooner we start, the sooner we's finished."

Then Hunter started. "Hey!" he said to Nana Rose, "I know you! I remember your house! You were really nice; I liked it there."

"Yes," said Nana Rose, obviously pleased. "And haven't you grown? You were knee-high to a grasshopper when you last came to my house.

I'm your mother's grandma; your Nana, and I used to take care of you as best I could. Before that, I took care of your mama, and her mama before that. By the time you came along, I was pretty old to be looking after young ones, but somebody had to do it. I used to worry so about what would happen to you when I died. But I see you've been doing a good job of growing, anyway." She turned to Faith. "You were just a baby when I died, but I did get to hold and rock you some. I wasn't much for singing to babies by then, but I did try."

She turned to introduce the others. "This," she said, pointing to the bald fellow with the pipe, "is your Grandpa, the Reverend Green. He's Helen's father, dead just since last March. I expect Helen's still missing him quite a bit, but at least he can be closer now then when he was living in Iowa and she here in British Columbia." She turned to the stout, old-fashioned woman next. "This is your Uroma Mika, last seen alive in 1912, before the first Great War when the Mika family left Poland for Germany. Technically, I guess she'd be your Ur-Ur-Uroma; something like that. She was a wise woman in her time, one of the last to know and gather the medicine plants and to doctor the people of her little town. It don't take much to see that she's the great-great-grandmother of Antonia, your new Mutti."

"And I'm Uncle Pete," said the fourth figure, "from Nova Scotia. Fished off Cape Breton. I'm Roger's father's father's father's second cousin, once removed. "

"But aren't ancestors supposed to be grandparents?" asked Hunter. "And how come there's nobody here related to my dad?"

Uncle Pete bristled. "You take what you can get! Do you think we just sit on our arses in the clouds all day, waitin' for you to call? Hell no, it's busy for us Maritimers. We had us some big families, and most of the fathers are lookin' after three or four dozen descendants by the time they've barely cooled in their graves. And we only hang around for a generation or two before we go back to start again as babies. I just happened to be between gigs, and available. Do you know how unusual a team of this size is? Let's see some gratitude, boy!"

He said "boy" like it was "buy," and the ups and downs of his voice were like swells of the sea. Hunter couldn't help liking the sound of it, even though he was disappointed at the poor showing of his own paternal line. And there was at least Nana Rose, whom he even remembered as a living great-grandmother; that was more than Faith could say.

"Okay," said Hunter. "Why are you here?"

The four looked at each other, then at the children. "Well," said Grandpa Green, "for you two, I guess. We aren't exactly told what we'll be needed to do, only that you need some, uh, help. Some guidance, I guess you'd say."

Faith rolled her eyes. "Great! More guidance! That's our problem—too many people guiding us! Why would anybody send us more?" Hunter silently agreed. After all, they weren't babies anymore; he was eleven and already knew most of what he needed to know to take care of them. He just needed to wait until he was sixteen, when he could legally drive and work. But guidance? No, thank you. He'd had enough of that to last him a lifetime.

"We'll see," said Nana Rose, and the others nodded.

Oma Mika then spoke up. "You could start with this room—I've seen pigsties that were tidier. Even if you kept goats in here, like I did in my house, you'd need to have some order. And what's that on the floor? Glass? Oh, my heavens! Somebody's going to get hurt that way. Get yourselves a broom and get started!"

"That's Faith's job," said Hunter. "It's her room."

"But Hunter left the cup in here, and if he hadn't left it here it wouldn't have broken!" protested Faith. "Why should I clean up what he left here?"

"Because you threw it!" said Hunter.

"But that was because Toni was yelling at me and telling me what to do!" yelled Faith.

"Enough!" said Oma Mika. "Faith, you sweep it. Hunter, you get the dust pan. Because if you don't it's Roscoe's paws that will be bleeding, and you'll both be sorry."

Grumbling, the children set to work. When they finished, the little people were gone, the dresser-top once again empty except for some pieces of paper, a pencil, an orange peel and some marbles Faith had left there.

"Do you think they'll come back?" asked Faith.

"Probably not," said Hunter. "Not after your complaining. Mutti keeps telling you to stop that."

Faith felt sorry for just a moment. She kind of liked the ancestors. Then, the old anger came back. She threw a bouncy ball at Hunter, who ducked and let it hit the wall. "Get out of my room." she said.

When he left, Roscoe did too. Faith almost felt like crying. "Why did they come, anyway," she muttered to herself, "just to disappear again, like everything and everybody else?"

Chapter 4: A Breaking Storm

Hunter knew that there was a fight brewing, and, although the ancestors may have distracted Faith from it for a day, the peace wouldn't last long. By four-thirty the next day, it was over.

Faith was standing on the stairway. Her eyes showed no emotion, but her chin jutted out and her jaw muscles looked tight. She reminded Hunter of a pit bull terrier. He rolled his eyes and muttered, "oh, boy—here it comes!" "Faith, your clothes are still on the floor, with the dirty and clean mixed up together. You need to sort them, bring the dirty ones to the laundry room, and fold the clean ones and put them away. Once that is done, you can go play." Helen was holding on to her "I'm being reasonable here" voice, but the slightly elevated pitch told Hunter that she had already said these things at least once. Faith stood stock still, blocking the stairway and making no move to do what she was told. Hunter moved past her to get to his room, as if he could hide from the coming storm.

Minutes passed, and Faith remained on the stairs. Then, with no response from Helen, she moved toward the coat hooks and picked up her jacket. Helen was quick, and snapped up Faith's shoes, lying in the doorway, before Faith could get them. "You're going nowhere, Missy."

Faith went for her gum boots, but when she sat on the step and raised the first boot to put it on, Helen grabbed the sole and pulled it out of Faith's hands. Faith reached for the second boot, and Helen put down the first to take the second from Faith. But when Helen put one boot down to grab the other, Faith would snatch up the one just released and attempt to put it on. Around and around like this went the boots, first to Faith and then to Helen and back, neither giving in but neither winning the battle, either. Faith began to scream at the top of her lungs; maybe that would drive Helen away. There were no words, just fury and determination. Then, as Helen reached for the boot that was almost on Faith's right foot, the foot pushed unexpectedly forward and hit, boot and all, Helen's face.

Now Helen was yelling too, in pain. Tears ran down her cheeks as her hand covered her nose, which had taken the blow full-on. She pointed up the stairs, past Faith, and yelled, "Go to your room! I don't want to see you!"

"Good!" shouted Faith in return. "I don't want to see you, either! You should have left me alone! I hate you! I hate it here! I never even wanted to move here in the first place."

"Go!" said Helen, sounding dangerous.

"I'm going!" Faith replied, "I'm going out and I'm not coming back!" She tried again for her boots and the door.

This time, Helen did not block her, and Faith was out the door. She would have stayed out, too, if she had remembered to grab her jacket. An early Autumn storm was under way, and the driving, cold rain stung on her bare arms. Her clothes were quickly getting soaked as she walked around to behind the house, and waited in the woodshed for a chance to go back in unnoticed.

"Cold?" asked a voice, and Faith turned to see Uncle Pete, warming himself on a transparent woodstove. "Sorry this can't help you more. You'll need a jacket or blanket soon."

"Yes, well it's her fault," said Faith. "She wants me to freeze. If she just let me go in the first place, I wouldn't be without a coat like this. Besides, my coat doesn't even fit, and I bet she won't buy me a new one."

"Have you told her it doesn't fit?"

"No. She's got eyes."

"And they are busy eyes, from what I've seen. You and Hunter take a lot of watching—especially you. I've seen you go over that windowsill. Not a bad jump, you make there—though I reckon maybe it stings a bit when you land," observed Uncle Pete.

"Thanks. It doesn't—sting, that is. And I'm not cold, either. This is nothin'." Faith noticed with annoyance that she was starting to talk like Helen, dropping the "g" at the end of words like an American. "You should have seen my first house—we didn't even have any heat when the wood ran out."

"You remember that far back, eh? Most people think you've forgotten your first parents."

"No, just because I was little doesn't mean I've forgotten everything. Hunter thinks he's so great because he remembers it, and he doesn't think I do. But I do remember being cold when the wood ran out."

"I wonder why they didn't just bring in more wood?" asked Uncle Pete, innocently.

"Because Roxanne wasn't there and Roger was asleep," replied Faith.

"Then what happened?"

"Then Hunter brought some in and tried to start the fire but he couldn't. And then Auntie Rhonda called, and she asked to talk to our mum and Hunter said she wasn't there, and then she wanted him to wake up Roger and we couldn't." Faith was surprised to find there were tears on her face. The words tumbled out. "And then the police came to take us. And Hunter hid us but they woke up Roger and he got into a fight with one. And they took him in handcuffs and we came out to see and they took us away, too. It wasn't even fair, because if our mum had of been there, she wouldn't have let them do it. And then we went to the Martins. But I do, too, remember."

"Sounds like a bad day all around," said Pete. "Was it pissin' rain, too, like now?"

"You aren't supposed to say 'piss'! You are a grown up!" protested Faith. But as she did, a funny thing happened to Pete. He got shorter, and even skinnier than he was. His rough face softened, his whiskers disappeared. He was a boy, in long rolled up pants, too-large boots without socks and a worn out plain woolen shirt. He looked about her age, and although he was grinning at her, she thought he looked sad somehow; watchful and jumpy.

"I'm a grown-up, a kid, and a baby. I'm no age at all, and every age a person can be. Do you think that ghosts stay the same age they were when they died? No, indeed—that's just life time. Dead time is different, slipperier. Makes it easier to remember things." He aged again, to a youngish adult. "I never was one much for polite language, not at any age. That's for the important people; the ones what's put on airs. Not for a workin' sod like me. 'Piss' is just a word, like 'dog' and 'fart.' I say what I mean; life ain't long enough to do anything else."

"Yeah, it was rainin'," admitted Faith, with the beginning of a shiver. It really was getting cold, and she sure wished Uncle Pete's stove could warm her, too.

"Well, maybe you'd best be getting' inside. I'll tell ya when the coast is clear. Listen, I'll whistle for ya."

Uncle Pete disappeared, and a few minutes later Faith heard the all-clear signal. She dashed to the front door, then opened it and slipped in as quietly as she could. Roscoe was waiting, and followed her upstairs, where she put on her bathrobe and gradually became warm.

She hadn't gotten past the keen ears of Hunter, however, and in a few minutes he was at her door.

Chapter 5: Coming Down a Peg

"You should knock," she said, as Hunter entered.

"Sorry. Where were you?"

"Just in the back. Hey, did you know ghosts could change their age?" Faith was eager to talk about anything except Helen and the fight downstairs.

"No, but did you know Helen's nose was bleeding? You shouldn't have done that, you know. What if they send us away?"

"I don't care. Maybe we can go back to the Martins."

"No, Faith, you know that we can't. This is about as good as it gets. Trust me, you don't want to stay in foster care forever. The Greens are adopting us; that's better than being moved around. Why can't you just get along for a few years until it's over and you are grown up?"

Faith looked her brother in the eye. "I know you're planning to leave when you're sixteen, but what about me? I'll have to stay. This sucks. I'd rather go back to Roxanne than live here."

"No, you wouldn't," said Hunter. "She might let you do whatever you want to do, but there wasn't even food there half the time. She can't take care of a fish, let alone kids. But anyway, why did you kick Helen? You're going to get us in so much trouble." Hunter shook his head as though he still could not believe what he had seen.

Faith felt something deep in her tummy. Was it hunger? Probably. She still had not eaten since she got home from school. But something else, too. Heavy and scared beneath the hunger. She wasn't angry anymore. It was a feeling like waiting for something very, very bad to happen.

"Yep, Missy, I'd paddle your behind for sure," stated Nana Rose. Shocked, Faith spun around to glare at the little woman. Then the others joined in.

"Spank her!" agreed Grandpa Green.

"Send her out to cut a switch and she wouldn't sit down for a week!" said Pete.

"Spare the rod and spoil the child, that's what I heard."

"Bring her down a peg."

Only Oma Mika didn't join in, but thoughtfully stirred a soup pot on the little stove. She was the age of a young mother today. Pete was still a boy, Grandpa Green looked about thirty. Nana Rose still looked old. Roscoe put his head between his paws.

"Are you talking about Helen hitting Faith?" asked Hunter, incredulously. "That's illegal, isn't it? You can't hit a child; that's child abuse."

Uncle Pete actually hooted. "Child abuse! For paddling a smart-mouthed kid who kicks you in the face? You think you've been around, boy? Huh, not much."

"Pete! What are you going on about? You are full of yourself!" said Oma. Gentler, she turned to Hunter, "Lots of people in my day spanked children. They even beat them. They had a saying, 'spare the rod and spoil the child.' But I didn't like to spank. It didn't do any good. I was afraid it would turn children into the kind of brutes that were always running people off their property in those days. Let the Tsars and the Kings and the Kaisers make children into soldiers, but I wasn't going to help them do it. Besides," she said, turning to the other ancestors, "don't any of you remember what it was like to be spanked? I mean, we were all children once." At that, she turned into a little girl with red curls and a dimpled smile, all big eyes and innocence.

"But sometimes you have to spank a child," said Grandpa Green, sounding both serious and a little bit unsure, as though convincing himself. "Otherwise they think that they are in charge, and not you. A child needs to know that the parents are in charge."

"Why?" asked Faith. She'd never wanted anybody to be in charge of her except herself, and maybe Hunter. Between the two of them, hadn't they done a better job than any adults could?

"Well, because if a child is in charge, then that child isn't safe," said Nana Rose. "I grew up on the edge of the wilderness, and so did my children. There were cougars, and flooding rivers, and even outlaws. If I said, 'get along home', they needed to go home, right then, and bar the door—no time to stop and argue about it."

Faith wasn't convinced. Surely she knew enough to run from a cougar.

"And a child in charge is a frightened child," added Oma Mika. "They don't have anybody bigger or wiser to count on. If you are only eight years old, but you are the smartest person around, well, that must be pretty scary."

Faith turned her jaw into iron and her eyes glared; it was her toughest look. No way was she admitting that Oma had a point. It was scary sometimes, having to know everything yourself. There wasn't time to learn everything. But adults weren't the answer; they were unpredictable, and they could be mean and hurt you or kick you out of their house. Come to think of it, adults were the main dangers that she needed protection against—they were more problem than solution.

As if she read Faith's mind, Oma Mika continued. "But to strike a child, especially a child who has been frightened or beaten in the past, is dangerous. The child might just decide that this adult is the problem, not the solution. The child can lose trust in all adults, forever."

The others nodded or looked at their feet in agreement. "Well," said Grandpa Green, "I see your point. It might be difficult, but Hunter and Faith's parents will have to find another way to be in charge, without spanking."

"Yup," agreed Uncle Pete. "Though I'd sure be wantin' to give 'em a smack, now and then. This little one can get pretty mouthy." He pointed his thumb at Faith.

There was a knock. "Faith?" Helen was at the door.

Faith panicked and slid under the desk.

"Faith?" Helen entered, looking around. Hunter scooted out the door. Faith held her breath. A marble rolled across the floor, out from under the desk and toward Helen. There, inches from her nose, was Grandpa Green, striking a bowler's pose. Faith gritted her teeth—Grandpa Green was giving her away!

"There you are! Come out. We need to talk."

Faith scooted out, but refused to look at Helen.

"Well," said Helen, "I'm still kind of mad, but I'm cooling down some. What got into you? Look at my face!"

Faith took a quick look, then looked away. Helen's face was already turning purple around the eyes and nose, like a raccoon. What would people say? What would Toni do? Faith felt a rush of emotions at once—fear, dread, anger, a little bit of pride and a tiny thrill of some sort. She'd really done a number! This never happened at the Martins. Maybe Helen and Tony really would send her back to them. Or maybe they would punish her in some awful way she'd never even heard of.

"I need to hear that you are sorry," said Helen.

Faith said nothing.

"I need to hear that you are sorry and willing to fix the damage to our relationship. I can see that you are not ready to tell me that, or to make amends. And until you are, you need to stay in your room."

"No problem," mumbled Faith. She had no idea what Helen even meant by "the damage to our relationship." It was Helen's face that needed fixed, and how was she supposed to do that? It made her mad all over again that Helen said things she didn't understand.

But when Helen left, Faith was alone. The ancestors were gone, too. There was just herself, and she was starting to feel something else beneath the fear of when Toni got home. Did she want to be invisible so that Toni couldn't hurt her, or because she was ashamed of what she had done? How did Helen do this—make her feel ashamed? Did she purposely go around making kids feel guilty? Or was this Faith's own feelings, something Helen didn't do to her, but that just came from somewhere within her?

She couldn't see the ancestors, but as the hot tears traced her cheeks, she heard a whisper.

"Atta girl," said a soft woman's voice, not old and crackly but young, familiar and dear. It was Nana Rose. "You go ahead and cry. It's a good thing to do, and brave in its own way. You had really hard day."

Faith got out a piece of paper and her crayons, and began to draw. She drew herself, with her foot and boot in the air. And she drew Helen's surprised face, getting a kick. She drew red lines out from the point of contact, to show the power, the shock and the pain of the foot hitting the face. She drew Roscoe, watching the scene, and a thought bubble saying, "Oh no!" Finally, she drew tears, first on Helen's face, and then on her own. At the bottom of the drawing, she wrote, "I'm sorry I kicked you." She folded the picture in half, and slipped it under Toni and Helen's bedroom door. They would find it there, later.

Suddenly, she was very, very tried. She lay on her own bed and slept, with her clothes still on.

Chapter 6: It's a Good Thing

Faith was dreaming. She was on a windswept shore, and the Martins were in a rowboat without oars, getting swept further and further from her. She was crying for them, but the water was cold and wild. Rain pelted down. Suddenly, someone grabbed her from behind and pushed her into a patch of earth, face down. She was pinned down, and she couldn't breathe. She pushed her head up and screamed with all of her might.

As the sound of her own shouts woke her, she found Roscoe licking her face. She reached out to him, by her bed, wagging his tail for her and savoring the salt on her cheeks.

"Ancestors?" she called softly, but there was no answer. Then, against her wall, she saw a huge shadow, hunched over like a monster with arms reaching toward her. She screamed in spite of herself.

Feet rushed down the hallway. The door opened, and Helen was framed in the hallway light. Behind her was Toni.

"Faith, honey, it's okay," said Helen. "You're ok." The small light went on by her bed, and Faith sat up. She was still crying, and the sight of Helen's face, still like a raccoon's with its two black eyes, made her cry harder. Toni sat beside Faith and pulled her close, rubbing her back. It felt good, and Faith wanted to give in to it and be held. But when she looked up at Helen, she stiffened. It was no use letting herself get comfortable now; now, when she would surely be sent away.

"Are you hungry?" asked Helen, unexpectedly. To her surprise, Faith found that she was. "I didn't mean you had to go to bed without supper," said Helen. "I thought you would come down before now and ask for something. When I came up to check, you had gone to sleep. Maybe I should have woken you up ...Well, anyway, are you?"

"Yes."

"Let's go down to the kitchen, then," said Toni.

In the kitchen, they heated some baked macaroni and cheese with broccoli, and with a slice of Toni's bread it tasted really good in spite of the sneaky vegetable. Faith could barely remember it now, but she knew she had once eaten macaroni raw from the cupboard at night when she was hungry. This was definitely better. When her stomach was more comfortable, she asked the one question that she knew couldn't wait until morning.

"So, where will I live now?"

"What do you mean?" asked Toni.

"Well, did you tell the Martins what I did? Will they take me back? Or do I have to go somewhere else?" asked Faith.

"Honey," said Helen, "this isn't foster care. You are staying right here with us. We adopted you, remember?"

"Well, yes, but ..." Faith trailed off.

"Do you remember when we had the ceremony here, and the Martins came, and your social worker from foster care, and the adoption worker?" asked Helen.

"Yes."

Helen pointed to a framed piece of writing on the wall. "Read that to me."

"On the adoption of Faith Sanford and Hunter Anderson, by Antonia and Helen Green. We, Antonia and Helen, promise to be forever parents to Faith and Hunter, to guide and to protect them, to take care of them until they are grown, and to be family to them as long as we live."

"So, where in there does it say, 'unless they screw up, in which case we will give them back?'" asked Helen.

"Nowhere."

"That's right. Giving you back isn't an option; you are ours. We may drive each other crazy sometimes, but that's part of what families are for. To get driven crazy by, and to know that even when you are behaving as rotten as you possibly can, you've got somebody to love you and help make it better. Understand?"

Faith didn't understand. The words were fine, but something was missing. This thing called family—no, it was this thing called parents—it didn't make any sense to her at all. What, she wondered, was the point of parents? How did anybody ever learn to understand them?

But she thought that maybe, just maybe, she was feeling a little bit better.

"Oh, I made you something."

"I know. I found it," said Helen. "I'm glad to know that you are sorry. I was worried."

"Worried about your face?" asked Faith, confused.

"No, worried about you. My face will get better. How are you doing?"

"Okay I guess," said Faith.

"You look confused," said Helen. "What a lot of enormous feelings you have in there! It must be so hard for you!" Her voice sounded sad for her, and kind.

Faith still looked blankly at Helen. She didn't want to think about what had happened, but she was starting to feel sorry about kicking Helen. "I'm sorry," she muttered.

Helen's face was soft, as she said, "It's been a hard day. I was afraid you would just stay mad all week! That would have been hard, too!"

A tear rolled down Faith's cheek. Helen went on.

"When you feel bad like that, I know it's hard. Lots of people get angry at the person they hurt, because they think that person is making them feel bad! But it's not me making you feel bad, it comes from inside. It's like your heart. It teaches you right from wrong. And I'm so, so glad that you have one. Things are going to be okay."

Faith looked at her blankly. No, parents definitely made no sense whatsoever. Still …

"Will you help me with this?" asked Helen. She held up a tube of cream. "It's for my face."

"Yeah, sure," said Faith. "And, did you put ice on the bruises?"

"Yep; I guess you know how to treat bruises!"

"Ruby taught me," said Faith. She very gently applied cream to Helen's face. "Frozen peas work good. Shall I get you some?"

"No, thank you. I'm about all iced out," said Helen. "I think these bruises will last a week or more, but the cream helps."

"Can I go to sleep in your room?" she asked. Faith didn't want to be alone, and somehow she knew the ancestors weren't coming back tonight.

"Sure, we've got room," said Toni. "Bring your blanket, and Roscoe sleeps with us anyway. Or he did, until you came along." She was smiling.

Faith went to get her blanket. Just as she turned out the light to leave, she heard Grandpa Green's voice soft in the dark. "Sorry about the fright, my girl," he said. "I'll show you how to make shadow pictures yourself some night."

So Grandpa Green had tricked her into screaming. Why? To be mean? No, he wasn't mean. Was it to bring Toni and Helen running?

"Yep," said Grandpa Green, reading her thoughts. "You may not understand 'em, but every kids needs 'em. You've got parents now, kiddo, and it's a good thing."

Chapter 7: Hunter's Secret

"I'm stopping at the grocery store," said Helen on the way home from school. "I have to pick up prescriptions, too, so it will take a little while. You guys want to go to the library?"

"Yes!" Hunter and Faith chimed with enthusiasm.

"I'll meet you over there, then," said Helen, dropping them off.

Faith headed to the children's section, while Hunter scouted out a computer terminal. He entered his Facepage ID and password. There were a couple of messages from friends at his old school, and a post from his cousin Sam. He joined a group for saving dolphins because Jeanette from school suggested it. Then he saw it; his heart leapt. To think he'd almost missed it! It was a friend request, from Gary Simms. His father!

"Hey!" said Faith, now standing behind him, and he jumped a foot out of his seat. Where did she come from, and how could she sneak up on him like that? "You aren't allowed on Facepage. Toni and Helen say you aren't old enough. And don't you have to be 18 to have a Facepage account? Isn't it illegal?"

"Don't tell!" said Hunter, desperately. "It's okay; all my friends do it. Their parents must let them. You just have to say that you are fourteen. Look, I'll show you how to do it, and then you don't tell on me and I won't tell on you."

"Well," Faith paused for dramatic effect, "I don't know. I'll have to think about it. Hey! That's Gary, your dad!"

"I know, idiot! Look, you have to promise not to tell. Tell you what, you can have all of my Pokemon cards, and I'll show you how to get on Facepage yourself."

"Hmmm, I'm thinking …"

"And I will buy you a candy bar. Any one you want."

"Okay. Deal. What'cha gonna do? Write to him?"

"Yes, of course! He's my dad! What am I supposed to do, ignore him?"

"Hmm … Helen would be really mad if she knew. We aren't supposed to go writing to people without her knowing."

"Why not?"

"Because, there's some paper all of our parents and grandparents have to sign before they can talk to us, and I heard Toni and Helen say that anybody who wants to contact us has to go through them. Like, have lunch with them or something."

"Lunch?" asked Hunter.

"Yeah, that's what I heard. I couldn't exactly ask why, since I was, like, on the stairs."

"Eavesdropping."

"No! Just hearing! I don't eavesdrop."

"Yes, you do. You're doing it now."

"I am not!"

"You are too. You're reading over my shoulder."

"I wasn't! I just came over to see what you were doing."

"Well, what I was doing didn't concern you." They glared at one another, then Hunter remembered that she had something to tell on him.

"Oh, never mind. Anyway, he's my dad, not Helen's or Toni's. I think I have a right to talk to him."

Faith settled herself in a chair next to his right elbow as he accepted the "friend" invitation. Together, they looked at Gary's profile. There was a picture of him, looking like Hunter remembered except a bit pudgier around the stomach and with longer hair. His hair was nearly to his shoulders, sandy-coloured and thinning. He had a mustache but no beard.

"Do you think I'll look like him?" asked Hunter.

"No way." Faith couldn't imagine Hunter looking like this guy—he was old! He looked like a hippy or something. Hunter liked to dress neatly, with his hair short and his shirt tucked in. One look at Gary, and Faith didn't like him at all.

"I think I might. He's tall, you know, and so am I. And we have the same hair colour."

"I don't think you'd want to," said Faith.

But Hunter was still excited. His dad wanted to contact him! He probably wanted to see him! He wrote his father a message.

"Hi, Dad. This is Hunter. I've been adopted by the Greens, did you know that? Faith, too. I'm eleven, and I've started training for football. Maybe you could come for a game. My team is going to be really good. Faith says hi, too."

"No, I don't," said Faith. Hunter erased the last line and sent the note. "Okay, show me how now," demanded Faith, "and don't forget the candy bar."

Hunter sighed. Sisters!

It was two days before he was able to check his site again. This time he was at his friend Anil's house. Sure enough, there was an answer.

"Hi, Hunter. When is your next game? I'd like to come. And be quiet about it. It's our secret."

Hunter eagerly wrote in the time and place for the following Sunday's game. He tried to tell himself that he wasn't excited, and that it probably wouldn't happen. He played a car racing video game against Anil with great intensity, almost losing his temper when he was edged off the track and his car blew up.

At practice on Thursday, Hunter worked like he had never worked before in his life. He could hear his coach saying, "that's it, Hunter! Throw you heart into it!" and that made him proud. But most of all, he could picture his dad being proud, and that made him hit the pads hard and push past the other players on the line, running across the yard line with one player hanging onto each foot and another closing in. Coach Jerry clapped him on the shoulder after practice, saying "play that hard on Sunday and you'll be starting every game this season." Hunter could hardly wait.

Sunday came, and Hunter searched the stands. Toni, Helen and Faith were all there. Even the Martins – George and Ruby – came with their stadium chairs. Ruby looked like she was waving an invisible little flag back and forth, cheering. The four adults sat in a clump, and Faith walked along the field edge, back and forth with the action. But Gary was nowhere to be seen. Maybe he's just not being obvious, thought Hunter. After all, Gary hadn't met with Helen and Toni, and so he wasn't supposed to be in touch with Hunter, or showing up where Hunter was. Hunter was sure that Gary was the kind of guy who hated big dramatic scenes; Hunter hated them himself. So, he must be sitting in his car or something, he told himself, and he played hard, imagining Gary out there, watching.

But after the game, which they lost by two points, Hunter had to admit to himself that Gary hadn't shown. At home, he showered and then retreated to his room, fighting the tears that brimmed up and threatened to expose his disappointment, and his foolish hope, to the others.

Chapter 8: After the Game

He should have known the ancestors would be making an appearance. Grandpa Green was even in his old football gear. "When is that from?" Hunter asked, eyeing the leather helmet.

"Nineteen forty-three. My first team, the Mount Morris Lions. I was fourteen; a defensive lineman. Later, I played for Eureka College, and Texas Christian University. I wasn't too bad in my day."

Hunter was impressed.

"Nice game, kiddo," said Grandpa Green.

"Thanks."

"So, why the dark cloud? Losing a game isn't important, especially this early in the season. You played well."

"No, it isn't that." Hunter looked away.

"It's that father thing," said Uncle Pete. "Can't you tell? He was hoping somebody would show up and he didn't."

Hunter glared at Uncle Pete. How did he know these things?

"Oh, I know how you feel about it. The Reverend over there don't know what it means to be without a father; he always had one," said Uncle Pete.

"Well, you've got a Heavenly Father!" said Grandpa Green. "Did you know that the Ancient Romans put a lot of stock in who everybody's father was? Your whole status in society depended on it. But Jesus' followers walked away from all of that. It didn't matter to them if their fathers were Roman officials, or Hebrew fishermen, or tax collectors—they all claimed only one Father in Heaven, and that made them equals. I bet you didn't know that—it's part of how the early Christians got under the skin of the Romans. They were willing to get fed to the lions over that point."

Grandpa Green's love of history amazed and puzzled Hunter. How could anybody care so much about something so long ago? Right now, it seemed to Hunter that his Grandfather was simply changing the subject.

"Well, Reverend, I don't mean no disrespect," said Uncle Pete, "but if you think that who your father is stopped mattering back after the Romans got through with it, then you ain't never been to the Maritimes. Or anywhere else, I reckon, without a father to call your'un. You see, people with fathers carry themselves diff'rent. They don't mean to; they just do. Like somebody who can always say, 'my father says this', or 'my father can do that.' They know it so deep down that they don't even know that they know it; they're protected. And the ones that see it are the ones that don't have it. Like some kind of shield that we ain't got. You have to be one of us to understand."

"So, you didn't have a father?" asked Hunter.

"No more than you do. There was a guy, name of Jenson; folks said he was my father. But they didn't say it to his wife. And they didn't say it to his face, neither. He was a tough bastard, that one, but it didn't do me no good."

"But my father doesn't say he isn't," said Hunter.

"No, but you don't see him advertising that he is," replied Uncle Pete. "His ancestors didn't even show up. You don't even have his name. Admit it, boy, that's how you got me. I know yer disappointed, but ya gotta take what shows up."

"Hmm," said Grandpa Green.

"It's not your fault," said Oma Mika.

"I admit it's prejudice," said Nana Rose, "But if there is one thing on this earth that I cannot stand it is a man who goes around making women pregnant when he has no intension of playing father to the children he spawns. Salmon are one thing; they get along without parents fine. But people are another."

"But why don't I have a better father?" asked Hunter. "I mean, why didn't any one want me? I don't even know why I look like Gary— couldn't somebody else be my father? I don't get it." He was trying to hold on to his tears, but failing as they spilled hot down his cheeks. He felt five years old again, as he remembered watching his father leave the last time. He had said he'd come back, soon. Why did he say that? What was it that Hunter didn't understand? He ran his fist into his pillow, then eyed the wall. He didn't want to bring the adoptive mothers running, but he did want to hit something that really hurt.

"Are you asking what makes somebody your father?" asked Oma Mika.

"You don't know, do you?" said Nana Rose, gently.

"Whoo boy," said Uncle Pete, as Grandpa Green cleared his throat. "It's a technical question, ain't it?"

"Well," began Grandpa Green, "you see, it takes two cells to make a baby, one sperm cell and one egg. The sperm cell comes from the father, and it fertilizes the egg cell, which comes from the mother ..."

"Um, yeah," said Hunter, a little confused. "Like salmon, kind of, right? So, like the sperm gets kind of sprayed on the eggs."

"Whoo boy," said Uncle Pete, looking toward the ceiling. .

"Well," said Grandpa Green, "it's a little more complicated. But when two people love each other very much, and they get married ..."

"Love don't always have anything to do with it," interrupted Uncle Pete. "And marriage don't either. Two people come together and have sex—that's the truth of it. The sperm has to get to the egg, and the egg lives in the woman's body. So they have to have sex. It might be nice and gentle, or it might not. They might be married, or they might not. They might plan to make a baby, or they might make one without planning, or, in the feller's case, even caring whether a baby happens or not. And poof—there you are."

"So, who is the father if the people aren't married?" asked Hunter, as the truth started to dawn on him.

"The man that had sex with the woman," said Uncle Pete. "It's a sperm thing—whoever's sperm gets to the egg, well, that's the father."

"You mean, somebody is your father just because they had sex with your mother?" Now that he said it, Hunter felt stupid. Of course, he had sort of known it all along. But somehow he thought that getting to be somebody's father was more magical than that; that a person was tied to their father in some powerful way that couldn't be broken and that determined everything about the kind of man they would become. Was it really just a chance thing, having sex and that's all? There was one question that could answer it.

"What if the mother had sex with more than one person; then who is the dad?"

"The one whose sperm got there first, just at the time when the egg was ready," said Grandpa Green.Hunter wondered how a pastor knew about these things. Then he wondered how a fisherman, or anybody who wasn't a scientist, knew. Baby's came out of women—so how did people figure all this out about fathers and sex? It was really rather amazing when he thought about it.

"Of course," said Grandpa Green, "you could have an adopted father. That wouldn't be about sex; it would be about choosing."

"Them choosing you?" asked Hunter.

"Or you choosing them. Sometimes one person thinks of it first; sometimes the other one does. I don't see why you couldn't do the choosing, if you found somebody you thought could be like a father to you."

"But they wouldn't really be my father, even adopted," Hunter said sadly. "Because I already have two adopted parents, Toni and Helen."

"By the way," said Oma Mika. "I don't want to interrupt this father talk, but do all children call their parents by their first names these days? It never happened in my lifetime."

"Nor mine," said Nana Rose.

"Nor mine, neither," said Uncle Pete. "Not unless I was talkin' about that Jensen feller, who didn't deserve the title of 'father', and who didn't claim it, either."

"Well," said Grandpa Green, "a few really modern families did it in the 1960's, but I don't think it worked very well."

"So," said Oma Mika, "are we all agreed that it's time these children start practicing saying 'Mother', or 'Mum', or 'Mutti' or something?"

A chorus of "yes", "yup", and "yeah" replied in affirmation.

"Okay, okay, now back to the father issue," said Grandpa Green. "What is Hunter to do about that?"

"Well," said Uncle Pete, "you can't expect him to just walk up to somebody and say, 'be my dad'. It don't work that way. Those that have fathers have got something they aren't gonna give to those that don't so easily. And the boy's right—all the spots are taken up by women in his case. He's got more mothers than you can shake a stick at, and one foster dad that is willing to be a grandpa to him, but no father. And that's a shame."

Hunter felt the tears brimming again, and turned his head away. It wasn't fair. Now that he thought about it, he was angry at Gary for not showing up; not today and not for six years. Not when the social workers wrote to tell him about adoption, not when his new mothers asked to meet him, and not now. He wondered whether his father had even been there when he was born; maybe he and Roxanne had already broken up by then. And he, Hunter, had always believed the stories about his having to be away for jobs and being too busy.

Hunter had defended Gary, and had glowered when the Martins or the Greens said anything about his not being around. Hunter had always thought that a father was magically connected to his child, and would, in the end, come through for him. But it wasn't like that; it was just a sperm thing. No magic, no claiming, no choosing, nothing to count on. Uncle Pete was right; it had made him feel worthless, like something thrown away. But now they were saying that it was simple: Gary had sex with his mother, and didn't want to be a father to the baby. Just like that.

Nana Rose spoke. "You know, it weren't anything you did. Gary just didn't want the fatherhood. You could have been the biggest, strongest, smartest boy that ever lived and it wouldn't have made any difference."

"That's right," the others chimed in.

Hunter could finally see that they kind of had a point. But he still thought that maybe if he had been smarter or cuter or something, his dad would have changed his mind. And he still thought that maybe someday it could work out.

"This is not going to be an easy problem," said Grandpa Green. The others agreed.

"Can I have a list?" said Grandpa Green. "If you had a father, what would you want from him?"

"Well, I'd like his name," said Hunter.

"Not gonna happen," said Uncle Pete.

"What else?" asked Grandpa Green.

"Well, he should be big, and like to teach me things. He should be smart about something that I want to learn about, like football, or heavy metal music, or history. He should be fun, and funny. I guess he should just, y'know, really like me."

"Like you more than he likes other people? Like you in a special way?" asked Oma Mika.

"Well, yeah. Not like a teacher or a coach that likes everybody. Even if they are really smart, they aren't, like, y'know, your own. They belong to everybody. They aren't going to take you places, just you, or be there when you grow up."

"So they need to be related to you, probably," said Grandpa Green. "So they care about you for your whole life."

"Yes," said Hunter, softly. He wouldn't have put it that way, because he wouldn't have even thought to ask for that much. But now that somebody had said it, it was exactly what he wanted. He wanted somebody who would care about him, just him, more than they cared about anything or anyone else. He wanted somebody who would think he was wonderful, whatever he did. He didn't want to have to measure up or be something grand; he wanted somebody to love him.

Hunter wondered whether Toni or Helen could ever feel like that to him. It didn't seem very likely. He had always thought that it would be his father, Gary; not a woman.

Hunter's eyes stung, and he felt a heaviness in his chest. Then his stomach began to feel upset. Was he getting sick?

"How do you feel, Hunter?" asked Nana Rose.

"Not so good," said Hunter. "I think I'm getting the flu."

"Nope," said Uncle Pete. "That's no flu, boy. That's just plain, dumb sadness. Hits us all. It's the sadness of life."

"We called it grief," said Grandpa Green.

"We called it the shaft," said Nana Rose.

"We called it Kummer," said Oma Mika. "But it means the same thing."

Chapter 9: That Darn Baby

"Baby Max is coming!" sang out Toni on a Saturday morning. "Are we ready?"

"What's to get ready?" asked Hunter.

"Baby-proofing," said Helen. "I'm covering the electrical outlets, and picking up anything small that he could choke on. Things with small parts, or that you don't want him to get a hold of, should go up above where he can't reach."

"So I have to pick up my Lego?" whined Faith. "I'm in the middle of making something!"

"'Fraid so," said Helen. "But we can put your project in here." She handed Faith a plastic bin from the kitchen.

"But I have the pieces all sorted just the way I want them! I worked hard on this!" She showed Helen neat piles of different sized pieces on the floor.

"I'm sorry, Hon, but those just can't stay on the floor like that. Max will put them in his mouth. He doesn't know any better."

Faith began throwing the Lego pieces into the general bin, ignoring the small box for her project. "Then I might as well just throw it all into here," she said, angrily.

"Doesn't he have, like, a playpen or something?" asked Hunter.

"That would be a good idea, Hunter," said Toni. "But I'm afraid his mother doesn't like to use playpens, so he's not used to that. I think if she put him in a playpen, he'd cry and cry."

"That's dumb," declared Hunter. "Babies shouldn't just crawl around the floor putting things in their mouths and poking at electrical outlets."

Helen laughed. "They certainly should not! Babies take a lot of watching!"

"How does anybody get anything else done, then?" asked Faith, still mad. "It's not like the baby is the only one in the house."

"Good point," said Helen. "Very little gets done when there are babies in the house. It seems like all Melissa does is chase after Max all day, I'm sure. But he won't be little for very long. And we're helping out today by babysitting while she goes out for a yoga class. She needs a break."

Hunter and Faith exchanged glances; they knew exactly what one another was thinking. Melissa needing a break from Max was not their problem.

Max arrived a half hour later with his mother and an enormous bag of supplies: blanket, toys, snacks in little snap-top containers, a bottle, diapers, change pad, extra clothes, a swing that hung from the door-frame between the kitchen and family room, and even a special little chair that clamped onto the table edge so that he could sit and look at the family while he had his snack.

"How long is he staying?" asked Hunter. "All weekend?"

"Just a couple of hours," reassured Helen.

"Isn't he a love?" cooed Toni, taking him in her arms. As she removed his coat, Hunter thought it looked like she was unwrapping a Christmas present; like she could hardly wait to wonder over his little hands and tell him how wonderful he was. He glowered.

But Max apparently did not want to be Toni's Christmas present baby. He started to cry right away, reaching out for Melissa. As Toni struggled to remove his coat, his protests reached screaming heights, and Melissa looked seriously distressed too.

"Oh, this is awful!" said Melissa. "This is what happens when I try to go anywhere! He just won't let me out of his sight! What do I do?"

"It's okay," said a calm Toni. "It's the ten-month-old blues. It's stranger anxiety and separation protest; most babies do this, especially if they aren't used to their mama leaving. But he'll be all right once you're out the door; really he will."

Melissa didn't look convinced, but with a kiss and a goodbye, she headed out the door with Toni in charge of the writhing, screaming Max. Hunter and Faith watched with big eyes, waiting for Max to wriggle right out of Toni's arms and land on the floor. But he did not. Within a few minutes, Toni had his coat off and was distracting him with a set of plastic keys from the supply bag.

Soon, Max was cruising around the kitchen and family room, walking by holding on to one piece of furniture after another. Faith tried offering him a bright wooden toy cell phone, and was encouraged when he took it, smiled, and gave it back to her. He was kind of cute in his own way, Faith thought. But when she caught her brother's look out the corner of her eye, she felt disloyal and silly for being almost won over so easily. Max had charm, but it was only a matter of time, she supposed, before he pooped his pants and started crying.

Sure enough, Max pooped. He didn't cry, though. He just looked very serious for a minute, as though he was concentrating on a hard problem, and then he stank.

"Seriously, Max!" complained Faith, holding her nose. "What did you eat to smell like that?"

Toni carried him off to the bedroom, and returned him soon smelling like a sweet baby again. But now he had some other problem on his mind. He started to fuss. Faith could hear that it wasn't a real cry; just a sort of whining, pouting fuss, interrupted by squawks.. The word "cranky" came to her mind.

In a few minutes, Toni was back, picking Max up and asking if he was hungry. He didn't answer, of course, but continued to fuss while she headed to the kitchen where Helen had the little chair set up at the table.

Faith and Hunter watched from a safe distance as Helen fed Max mushed bananas with a spoon. It was an incredibly messy process. Sometimes, Max turned his head just as the spoon arrived, smearing bananas on his cheek. Other times, the spoon went right into his mouth and the bananas hit their target while Helen cheered as though Max had hit a home run or something. Then, as often as not, he spit the bananas back out! With as much mashed banana on Max as in him, Helen presented Max with his second course: a bowl of Cheerios.

If Max and the bananas were somewhat gross, Max and the Cheerios were appalling. He picked them up with his whole sticky little fist, which he then raised to his mouth. He tipped the bowl, spilling them onto the table and floor. Finally, he began pushing them off the table and onto the floor. First it was just a few, then more and more Cheerios and finally the bowl itself went flying off the table. By then, Faith had moved just close enough for Max to catch her eye and grin happily as he looked from the floor to the table and back again.

"Dat!" said Max, looking right at Faith and then leaning over and pointing to the floor. "Dat! Dat! Dat!" He was getting louder, and starting to cry. Faith, startled, went over to Max, picked up the bowl, and put it back on the table for him. He threw it off, then leaned over and cried for it again. Faith put it back; Max knocked it off. Faith put it back; Max knocked it off.

"Okay," said Faith, "this could get pretty tiresome after a while. You threw it on the floor; it stays on the floor."

Max cried, "Dat! Dat! Dat!" he said, and his eyes filled with big tears.

"Toni!" called Faith, "I'm not taking care of this baby!" She stomped off, followed closely by Hunter, to her room.

"What a brat!" Hunter declared in the privacy of the bedroom. "All he does is cry and make messes!"

"Oh, I don't know," said Faith, "I didn't think he was that bad. He was okay when he was walking around things. And he's kinda funny, like the way he gets all serious when he poops." She imitated Max pooping, with a look like she was listening to something far away followed by "pptthhh!" This sent both of them laughing, so she did it again. And again.

"Ppptthh!" came from the direction of the dresser-top.

"Hey, that wasn't me!" said Faith, looking directly at the ancestors who had gathered. It hadn't sounded like one of them, either.

Nana Rose was sitting in a kitchen chair today, with a baby holding on to her knees to balance itself on wobbly legs. "Ppptthh!" said the baby again. Nana Rose offered it a big wooden spoon, and down sat the baby to pound the floor with its new toy.

"A baby?" said Hunter, "A ghost baby? Who is it? I mean, who was it?"

"It's Faith," said Uncle Pete.

"But Faith is here; she's alive. How can she be a ghost?"

Grandpa Green chewed on his pipe getting ready to explain. "Well, you know that ghosts don't live in time the same way that living people do, right? We travel. Someday Faith will be a ghost. She'll travel, too, and she'll be whatever age she chooses. So she's travelled here, and she's a baby."

Hunter and Faith both nodded, pretending to understand. Neither wanted to show the ghosts that they were confused. This time-travel stuff was new.

"So, is this what I looked like as a baby?" asked Faith. The ghost baby had a bald head that looked too big for its body; just like Max did. It had on yellow stretchy pajamas with feet, and its diapered bottom was round and cushy-looking as it plopped from standing on its short, fat legs to sitting on the floor. When it crawled, that little bottom stuck up in the air just a little. When she looked closely at the little face, Faith thought that the baby's nose was about the same shape as its bum, but much smaller, and that made her smile. "I was kind of cute."

"Not really," said Hunter. He felt his mood slipping from glum to something else—what was it? Annoyance? Boredom?

"Can we do something else?" he asked.

"Like what?" replied Oma Mika.

"I don't know; like watch something," said Hunter. "A movie or something."

"We are not the entertainment," said Nana Rose firmly. "We're here to teach."

"But we can show you something," said Oma Mika. "Would you like to see yourself as a baby?"

"No!" Hunter surprised himself with how strongly that came out.

"But we saw me, we should see you, too!" whined Faith. "I want to see you as a baby. You saw me twice—when I was really a baby and now. We should see you."

"What'cha worried about, boy?" asked Uncle Pete. "'Fraid you were ugly or sompthin'?"

"No," said Hunter, feeling trapped. "I just don't want to."

But it was too late. Something was happening on the dresser-top, and it wasn't the ancestors. It was, in fact, rather like a movie, but in 3-D and with no other special effects. If this were a movie, thought Hunter, no one would come to see it.

There was a baby in a crib. His diaper was full under wet-footed pajamas. The blankets were bunched up, leaving the bare plastic top of the mattress exposed. His face was red, not only from crying but also from something that looked like a rash. He kept pulling himself up on the bars of the crib and plopping back down again, crying and crying. He turned and laid his head on the bare mattress, still crying.

Hunter didn't want to look, but he couldn't help it. How could he not look at a crying baby? He guessed that maybe that was why babies cry after all; to get somebody's attention. But this baby, he somehow knew, had been crying for a long time. He thought that the baby had a tummy ache from being hungry, and that the rash on its face and hands was also itching and burning under the pajamas and the wet, full diaper.

Hunter could not believe what was happening. It was like he remembered being that baby. He could feel its hurting tummy and skin, and something else—sadness. Terrible, terrible sadness. Then, his feeling changed to anger.

"What is wrong with those people?" he whisper-shouted between clenched teeth. "Why doesn't anybody pick up that baby? Can't they see that it's hungry and has a rash?" He felt his eyes stinging and his chest got heavy. He looked for something that he could kick or punch without making a noise that would draw the mothers to the room. Hot tears spilled down his cheeks. "What was wrong with them?" he asked again, "didn't they know it was time to pick me up? Where was everybody? Where was my mum?"

Hunter almost choked on the last word. He felt stupid, standing there crying with Faith watching him. He was angry at the ancestors, too. He didn't want to see that; why had they showed it to him? e sat, then rolled over onto Faith's bed, curling his body around a stomach that now ached as he turned his face to the wall.

Faith stood watching, wondering what to do. "Go tell your new mums," whispered Oma Mika, now at her ear. "Get some help."

Faith ran downstairs.

A minute later, Helen was at Hunter's side, while Toni stood in the doorway watching and holding little Max.

"What is it, Hunter?" asked Helen gently. "Tell me, please." Her voice was soft, and a little worried. "Are you hurt? Or sick?"

Hunter found that he had no words. He still had the picture in his mind, but the speaking part of his brain didn't seem to be working at all. Nor did he want to tell Helen about what he had seen.

"I think he remembered something, from when he was little," said Faith, "like Max's age."

Hunter held his breath. He just knew that Helen and Toni would not believe Faith; everybody knew that it was impossible to remember something from being a baby. But wasn't that exactly what had happened? It was like his body had remembered what it felt like, even though his mind had long ago forgotten the story or the pictures of what had happened to his baby self.

"Oh, wow!" said Helen softly. "That must have been really hard."

"It was a real memory, too," said Faith, "I'm sure of it."

"I believe so, too, Faith," said Helen. "I think we just have to wait a little bit for some words to come for Hunter to describe it. Maybe I can help." She was sitting on the bed. "Is it okay if I rub your back?"

"No," said Hunter. "Just my arms."

"Okay," said Helen. "I'm just going to rub your arm here. Will you tell me if I get it right?"

"A little harder," said Hunter. "No, just hold your hand still there." Helen's hand stopped moving but stayed with warm pressure on his arm. It felt okay there.

"Why didn't anybody come to pick me up when I was in my crib?" he asked. "I think that I was hungry and my skin hurt. But she didn't come, and didn't come. I cried and cried. I slept some, and then I cried again. But she didn't come."

"Oh, Hunter, that was so hard. You were just a baby, and you needed your mama to take care of you," Helen looked sad. "But she didn't come."

After quite a long time, Hunter sat up. "I wonder if that was really a memory," he said. "I wonder why my mum didn't come that time."

Helen looked thoughtful. "I think it's a real memory Hunter. When you were a baby, you came into foster care once with a bad rash all over your body. It happened because you were left too long in your crib, with wet pajamas and diaper. I know it's hard to understand how somebody could leave a baby so long without care like that, but your first mother had a bad addiction to drugs. Sometimes the drugs were the only thing that she could think about or care about for days on end, and you got left hungry and wet until she remembered again to take care of you."

"Is that what happened?" he asked. "I wondered." He looked at baby Max, who was still in Toni's arms in the doorway. "I can't imagine somebody leaving Max alone. He'd destroy the house!"

Toni smiled. "No, a baby probably wouldn't destroy the house. Especially if it was in a crib. But he'd sure raise a big noise! And no, I can't imagine leaving him alone, either. He's too precious to leave alone like that." Toni's face got sad, then, and she sighed heavily. "And you, too, Hunter. You were too precious to leave alone like that. You were precious like little Max here. I would sooo have picked you up!"

"Me, too!" said Helen. "In fact, I was thinking maybe you were hungry now. Like, for lunch."

Hunter was indeed hungry for lunch. Soon they were all around the table eating sandwiches and carrot sticks.

"Sorry, buddy," said Uncle Pete later on. "That was a hard thing to see. But it didn't stay that way for ya. You got a better spot now, and parents that don't have the addictions. They can love you, if you let 'em."

Chapter 10: Messing with Brains, and Nana Rose's Story

The autumn was passing by—school was in full swing, and Grandpa Green was giving Hunter football tips nearly every day. Faith helped Helen put healing cream on her face each evening at bedtime, and the dark bruises slowly disappeared. Toni took the children out into the forest on weekends to hunt for mushrooms. Faith, with a little help from Nana Rose, was becoming an expert at spotting Chanterelles, Oyster Mushrooms, Puffballs, and even Boletes and Pine Mushrooms, which were much harder to spot than the Chanterelles, that practically jumped out of the forest floor once you knew what to look for. Toni thought Faith was a genius at mushroom hunting, and Faith was pleased at this. If she ever needed to fend for herself, she thought, she'd do okay—especially if Nana Rose stuck around. Oma Mika seemed to enjoy these trips, as well, and asked Nana Rose many questions about the local plants. Oma Mika claimed to know a great deal about the plants in the part of Russia where she had lived, but found North American flora and fauna somewhat different. Faith listened carefully as the two women discussed what was edible, what was poisonous, and what was useful for which medicinal purpose.

One day when both of the children were along for the hunt, Hunter asked Toni if she knew how to find "magic mushrooms."

"What kind of magic do you mean?" she asked.

"You know, the ones that make you stoned," he replied.

"They are called psilocybin mushrooms, and, yes, they do grow around here. I myself have never learned to identify them. Some people have used them for visions; they cause hallucinations. But they can also make you really, really sick. Especially if you don't know what you're doing with them," said Toni.

"What are halluci—whatevers?" asked Faith.

"Hallucinations. Seeing, hearing or feeling things that aren't there," said Toni.

"Like ghosts?" said Hunter, giving Faith a wide-eyed, meaningful look.

"I guess so," said Toni. "Or just patterns, even. I think it depends a lot on the frame of mind a person is in—what they expect to see, whether they are calm or upset, and so on. And also whether they know the right amount to take, and how to prepare it. People who use psilocybin mushrooms for making visions would need to know a lot about it to do it safely."

"Why would somebody want to see or hear what isn't there?" asked Faith.

"Good question. In old times, some people thought that if they made visions happen, the ancestors would teach them things. But nowadays, I think a lot of people are just interested in them as a way to get high."

"You mean, stoned?"

"Yeah."

"Our mum gets stoned," said Faith. She was beginning to feel comfortable talking to Toni, in spite of herself. She noticed that Toni listened, asked questions, and knew a lot of things. Not as much as Oma and Nana, of course, but quite a few things. And ever since her nightmare, she was discovering that Toni could be nice to lean up against—very soft and warm.

Not that she was letting her guard down. It's fine, she thought, to just enjoy that feeling once in a while as long as I don't get too attached to it. So, every once in a while, she made sure that Toni knew she could take it, or leave it any time. It wasn't something that she thought she would ever actually need again—she wasn't a baby or anything.

"Yeah, she sure does" said Hunter. "Or, at least she did. She might be too sick to get stoned now."

"I wonder what if feels like," said Faith. "I bet it's fun, like this" and she began to walk crooked, laughing and bumping into things.

"Don't be stupid, Faith!" said Hunter. "It messes up your brain! And you get addicted, and do bad things. Drugs and alcohol pretty much ruined our family. I'm never going to do it, and trust me, Faith, you better not either. You'll be sorry".

Later, exercising Roscoe in the park across from their house, they brought up the topic again, this time with the ancestors. Outdoors, the ancestors sometimes turned up life-sized, walking along almost like living people.

"Here's what I wonder," said Hunter. "I thought people got stoned because their parents didn't' care. But Nana Rose, didn't you care about your kids? And didn't you take care of our mother, too? How come you took care of our mother, unless her Grandma Lily wasn't doing it very well? And how come she didn't do better, if she had you for a mother? And how come our mum got messed up with drugs and alcohol? Why didn't you stop her?"

"Whoo, boy," said Uncle Pete. "You do have a way of asking the hard questions."

"Well, yes," said Nana Rose, "but don't forget, Pete, that's what we're here for. To answer the hard questions."

"Yeah, but he's only eleven! How's he know so much about what to ask?"

"Come on, Pete," said Nana. "You'd been around from pillar to fence-post by the age of eleven. Don't tell me you didn't want to ask the same things!"

"Yeah, yeah, so yer right. Some of us learn early about things that others never do learn about." Here he gave a pointed look at Grandpa Green, who widened his eyes.

"I heard about just about every part of life in my ministry," said Grandpa Green. "Just because I didn't pick up a bottle myself doesn't mean I didn't know what went on. I wish all children could stay safe until they were grown up, but things happen and the kids always seem to get the worst of it."

"Well, what about my question?" said Hunter.

Nana Rose sat down on a bench and sighed.

"It's not so simple. No one ever looked into the eyes of their baby, and said, 'hey, I think I will just mess this one all up!' I'd have wrestled bears for my kids, swam rapids and stared down cougars. But those are the simple things. A mother knows what to do with a bear!"We lived in a time when families got caught in big problems, like drugs and alcohol, and coal mines, and wars, and logging."My father came over from Great Britain in 1880 to work in the coal mines of Nanaimo. That was a big settlement with people from all over the world—China, Britain, Ireland, Italy, even black people from the United States worked in the mines. A mine was like a pit going straight down into Hell. The big mine in Nanaimo blew up in 1887, killing 150 men, just like that. My father wasn't on that shift, thank the Lord.

"There was plenty of work then, with the building of a colony still in full swing. Mining and logging, too. We moved around like gypsies, going with the work. I got some schooling, but not much, and I learned how to take care of sickness and injuries—there wasn't any doctor or hospital around. Of six children, just two of my brothers and I made it past twenty years old, and that wasn't too bad; some families did worse.

"I married Tom and he worked for the logging camps. Tom was Salish Indian, but his village got moved when he was just a child, and he grew up in a Residential School. His parents died young, and we didn't see much of mine, either. He looked white, and since he worked for white men we sort of dropped the Salish part in time. But our children knew the animals and plants, and how to jig cod, bring up crabs, clean and smoke or pickle all kinds of fish, from halibut to trout."

"Wait!" interrupted Hunter. "Are you saying we're part Salish? Like, First Nations Salish?"

"Oh, yeah! You sure are! Part Salish, part Welsh, part Nova Scotian ..."

"Part German, part American," added Grandpa Green.

"Part Russian," added Oma Mika.

"Okay, okay, part everything!" said Faith. "Go on with the story!"

"Those were the heydays of the logging camps, all up and down Vancouver Island. People worked hard, played hard, fought hard and drank hard. They'd do anything for one another in emergencies, and there were plenty of those. But they'd kill each other with fightin' in between. The women gossiped and the men brawled! We were a pretty rough lot!

"Tom and I loved a good dance, and Tom didn't mind a good fight. But at home, we'd put on the radio and listen to a story, or dance together. Out our front door were tide pools, forests, rivers, the big trees, the birds—oh, the eagles! It was something. We'd build fires on the beach and eat mussels and clams until we thought we'd burst. We'd sing silly songs and tell stories. Except for the drinking and the brawls, It was a good life until the kids grew up."

"Then things got rough. Doug went off to war; he didn't come back. Grey died when his rope let go forty feet up a tree and he fell. Sal got through high school and went to work on the docks. Little Trinity died of pneumonia when we couldn't get out to the hospital and my doctorin' wasn't enough."Vi and Daisy settled in Victoria and looked after me when I was old. Not that I needed much looking after. Iris went back east with her husband, and they raised horses. Then, there was Lily. She met her husband while she was cooking in a logging camp, and the two of them drank far too much, if you ask me.

"Now, I know the boredom of those places, and the fear that the work puts into you. But that's no excuse for drinking during the day, or for leaving the children unattended at night. Lily's children would come and stay with me for weeks at a time, and I gave them all the love that I could. The boys were all right most of the time; boys are easy. But the daughter, Roxanne, was around drunken men from the time she was a baby, with no one awake to protect her. I think she got hurt bad. When the family moved into town for the kids to go to high school, Roxanne got into boyfriends, booze, and drugs. That just broke my heart."When Roxanne started having her own babies—that was you two—she brought them to me. She loved you, but she didn't seem to be able to think one minute ahead. I'd teach her things, like sewing and crafts, and anybody could tell she was smart as a whip. It was hard to understand how she could be so smart and yet not see ahead to what would happen if she didn't put aside the rent, or protect new kittens from raccoons, or build a proper coop for the chickens. She couldn't keep a job, either. She'd start out all hopeful, and then three weeks later it would come apart. And of course, there were still the boyfriends, booze and drugs. She had bad addictions. When I had you, you ate well and played outdoors with the neighbour children. But I didn't know what would happen to you when I died."

Hunter thought Nana Rose was being pretty easy on Roxanne. Nana Rose didn't seem to blame Roxanne for the things that had happened at all. "But, I'm the one who got beaten up by her creepy boyfriend, and taken into foster care, and had to look after Faith whether I wanted to or not," said Hunter. "You make it sound like that was nobody's fault at all."

"Maybe it wasn't one person's fault," said Nana Rose. "Or maybe you want to look at those men she kept picking—they weren't exactly great specimens of manhood. I'm just saying that it wasn't simple and I couldn't prevent it by myself."

"But you did use alcohol," said Faith. "You showed them how."

"Yes, I did. I wish I hadn't. I wish none of us had. I'm sorry, Faith and Hunter. Nowadays, we know better. Alcohol is poison to babies before they are born; it messes with their brains. Maybe that's why Roxanne can't think ahead; maybe it was Lily's drinking. And maybe Lily's brain didn't work as well as it could have, because by the time she was born, I was drinking every day, just a little, and a little more on Fridays." She sighed. "Well, I do apologize. It took three generations, but the price came down on you."

"What do you mean? What price?" asked Faith, alarmed. "Are our brains messed up?"

"I can't say, my dears," said Nana Rose. "If it wasn't for the alcohol, maybe school would be easier for you, Hunter. Maybe you wouldn't lose your notebook or forget your chores so often. And maybe Faith could keep her temper more easily. Maybe she would not have trouble sleeping through the night like she does. If mothers drink when they're pregnant, it changes the baby's brain. You can't undo the damage, and it will make some things difficult for you. You'll have to work harder, and so will your parents, in order to help you become the best that you can be."

Hunter felt sorry for Nana. He wanted to put an arm around her. She looked very old. He felt that she had watched Lily, then Roxanne, then him and Faith with that helpless look, and he wanted to tell her that it was alright now, after all. He would do what she wished she had; he would stay away from drugs and alcohol all his life.

Faith, however, looked right at Nana, as much in the eyes as one could with a transparent person. Then she looked at Hunter, wondering for a moment what he had meant about having to take care of her, and then back at Nana. Roxanne, she thought, was not the only one who had been defenseless, or had cruel things done to her. Roxanne should have to pay.

The other ghosts had listened, too. Now Oma Mika came and put her arm around Nana Rose. "It started long before you," she said. "Yours is just one part of the story. It started in the mines, and in the schools that they sent your husband's people to. And before that in wars, maybe, or in people getting moved off their lands. It's always hard for working people, and alcohol is one way the mine operators, and the army officers, and the ship captains bought the men off. We had troubles with it in Russia, too."

Uncle Pete just said, "aw, shite, that's the truth", and looked at his boots. Grandpa Green, not in his wingback chair but on a stool like the others, sighed sadly.

Now Nana got up, and brushed her hands together, as though getting ready to start a new loaf of bread. "Well, that was then," she said, "and this is now. Tell me, Faith, how are you going to fix those mushrooms we picked?"

"But wait a minute! What does happen now?" asked Faith.

"Well, now the cycle is broken," said Uncle Pete. "You won't make the same mistake; you can choose differently and not use drugs or alcohol."

"But what if I want to? She said it was fun, sometimes," persisted Faith.

"What! Haven't you been listening?" yelled Hunter. "Alcohol is what ruined everything! She even drank when she was pregnant! Are you crazy?"

Faith's face was hard in anger and concentration. "But Nana got to choose. Lily got to choose. Roxanne got to choose. They all got to drink alcohol and to have fun. They didn't have to pay. But I do, and I want to choose, too."

"Well, honey," said Grandpa Green, "you are right about one thing, and wrong about another. Each person does their own choosing, and you will do yours, too. But if you think that they didn't have to pay, then you are not paying attention. Your Nana had to love you as a baby and wonder who would raise you, and what kind of pain you were in for. She had to watch while her daughter and then her grandchildren became selfish and unhappy because of alcohol and drugs. And now your first mother Roxanne is sick, from all the drugs and alcohol ruining her liver and kidneys. That's what addiction does. The person starts to blame other people, and to be angry all the time. They can only think about the alcohol, or the drugs, and they lose sight of the important, wonderful things that God gave them and that could make them happy—like their children, for instance. Like you."

Faith felt tears behind her eyes, and that just made her angrier. These ancestors are all for letting people off the hook, she thought. My mother didn't care about us. She left us alone, and she let men hurt us, and she didn't even stop them. Faith thought that maybe she wanted to drink alcohol too, just to get even with Roxanne and to show Roxanne the bad that she had done. And, even though she had never tried it, she thought that being drunk was going to be fun; otherwise, nobody would do it.

Faith looked at Hunter, who was looking grumpy himself. "Well, I'll tell you one thing," he said to Faith, "I had to take care of you as a baby, and I had to take care of our mum too. But if you grow up to be a drunk, I'm not taking care of you again, and that's final."

Faith picked up a rock and threw it at a tree as hard as she could. That felt great! She picked up another.

"Do it again!" yelled Uncle Pete. "Again! Again! AGAIN!" cheered the four ancestors as she threw rock after rock. Hunter joined in with the throwing. "Find your own tree!" yelled Faith. She wasn't going to let this change into a competition; it was her rocks and her tree. So they each threw rocks while the ancestors cheered, until they were tired and spent and didn't need to anymore.

When the throwing was over, Faith felt so much lighter that she almost laughed. The ancestors were throwing, too, but they couldn't hit anything real with their ghost stones. Maybe that's why they cheered me so much, she thought. I bet they have their own stories that made them want to throw stones, too. And as long a she threw rocks at trees and not at people, she wouldn't even get into trouble for it.

Chapter 11: Smashed Fingers

That evening, around the supper table, the children were still thinking about all they had heard that afternoon.

"You should have seen these two gather mushrooms, Helen," said Toni. "They are quick learners! I couldn't believe it! I'm not sure I even told them about Oyster mushrooms, and Faith found a whole tree trunk of them!"

"They are my favorites," said Helen with her mouth half full. "Except for Morels, but those don't come until spring. I know who I'm sending out to look."

"You should come, too, Helen," said Hunter.

"Yes!" chimed in Faith. "It would be more fun if all five of us were there."

"Does Roscoe help? Is that the secret?" asked Helen.

"Not unless chasing squirrels somehow helps with mushroom spotting. Or maybe it cuts down on the competition," said Hunter.

"He helps!" said Faith, loyally. "And the an ..."

"And the ancestral knowledge of the woods that I got from my father!" cut in Hunter, giving Faith a 'be quiet' look.

The table was quiet for a moment. Then, abruptly, Faith brought up something that had bothered her from the afternoon. "Hunter said that he had to take care of me when we lived with Roxanne. I don't think he did."

"Did take care of you? Or did he have to?" asked Helen.

"Did have to. He could have just left me alone, like he does now," answered Faith, with just a bit of an accusing look in Hunter's direction.

"I don't just leave you alone! I play with you!" defended Hunter. "But then, if I had left you alone, you would have screamed all day and all night! You cried all the time! I couldn't leave you alone—I had no choice."

The two adults looked at each other, and again at the children. "What was it like, Hunter?" asked Toni.

"She was a really, really fussy baby. Geesh! And she wouldn't even stop."

"Well, did you try feeding me? Or changing my diaper?" Faith retorted. "Yes, and it didn't help. You just wanted our mum. I tried to give you a bottle of milk, and you'd drink it, and then you'd just scream again, even louder. I'd put you in your crib, and you would cry and scream and scream. Then, when you were not even one year old, you climbed out and fell! Then you would come after me!"

"It sounds like you didn't know how to make her happy," said Toni.

"That sounds like a terrible experience. I guess maybe that's why you don't like babies. Even Max. I think he's adorable, but to you, is he just another baby?" asked Helen.

"Yes."

"Then what happened? Didn't you like her more when she was old enough to play with?" asked Toni.

"No, not really. If our mum was home, or Roger, she would take up all of their attention. And if they were gone, she would follow me. She had the idea, and I don't know where she got it, that she belonged in every room in the house, and that everything in it was hers to play with. She would break my toys, and she even peed on my clothes and on my bed. Everything stunk like her pee! I would try to get away from her, but she would just stand outside the door to my room and scream to get in! There was nothing I could do to convince her that I didn't want to be with her. She'd follow me everywhere, and whine."

Faith was indignant. "I did not pee on your things! I was a baby, and baby's wear diapers. If I peed on things, it was because you didn't put a diaper on me."

"You did, too! And you took off diapers!" said Hunter. "I couldn't get away from you!"

Suddenly, tears sprung to Faith's eyes. "You shut the door on my fingers!" she said, softly. Toni reached quickly over to hook her arm around Faith, and pulled her to the front of her own chair, where Faith stood until her legs gave in and she landed on Toni's generous lap. She couldn't look at Toni, or anybody, but she felt Toni and then Helen, too, stroking her hair and rubbing her shoulders. She felt frozen, tears running down her hot cheeks. Her breathing stopped, until it came in something that sounded like, but could not be, sobs. She didn't even feel like Faith anymore. It was like she was small, so small, and all alone.

"Ouch!" said Toni. "That hurt soo bad! Let me see those fingers." She gently picked up Faith's hand, and kissed each finger. Then, just to be sure she had the right ones, she kissed the other handful of fingers, one by one.

Hunter, amazed, wondered what had just happened. He didn't remember shutting the door on Faith's fingers—had that really happened? He'd never seen Faith act like this, though. It wasn't like she looked when she was tattling on him. She just looked small, and sad, and confused. So, it must have happened. And that could only mean one thing—he was in trouble.

Helen turned toward him. Oh, boy, he thought, here it comes. He studied his plate. "I bet that was a pretty bad experience for both of you," she said, still sounding sad.

"After all, you were only about four or five years old, yourself."

Hunter risked a glance up at her. She looked sad, too, even as she looked right at him! Not angry, but sad. But that didn't make sense. If he smashed a little kid's fingers in the door, wasn't that going to get him in trouble?

Helen sat back down. Now they were all at the same level.

"So, let me see if I understand this. Do you remember the time Faith got her fingers caught in the door, Hunter?" began Helen.

"No."

"Well," she continued, "it makes sense that you wouldn't. You were just little yourself, and I don't imagine it's something that you wanted to think about very often! And if there was no adult around, then probably nobody talked about it again."

"But you were a little kid when you were brought back from foster care to live with Roxanne again. Faith was a new baby, and Roger was Roxanne's partner. Roxanne and Roger had been trying hard to stay clean and sober and to get the family together, but that didn't last, and now they were back to drinking and using drugs. So you were alone with the baby a lot, but you were only three, then four, then five years old. So little! Babies are a lot of work, even for grown-up mamas! You were too small even to warm up her bottle just right, and all you knew to feed her was cow's milk, right?"

"You mean, like milk milk?" asked Hunter, confused. "Yes, it comes from cows. I know that. But, like, what else is there?"

"Most tiny babies can't drink cow's milk straight from the fridge like that," explained Helen. "They need special baby formula, warmed up not too hot. Cow's milk makes their tummies hurt, sometimes really badly. Maybe that's why Faith couldn't stop screaming. And she missed her mama, too. The best food for little babies is breast milk"

The children's eyes were wide. Was Helen really talking about breasts? At the table? Toni kept cradling Faith, whose breathing was now slow and steady, but whose face was still red and tear-streaked. Hunter was still wary.

Helen continued "And if there isn't an adult to take really good care of them, babies stink! They can't help it. They need adults to change them and to wash them. If they don't get changed, then their bums get sore, and that's another reason why they cry and whine. They don't understand why they feel bad; they only know it hurts.

"You see, babies have sort of a built-in system to get big people to take care of them. For starters, they come out really cute, with big eyes and cute, squishy noses, like Max. That makes most people want to pick them up and carry them. And they have a loud, high-pitched, horrible cry that attracts help when they needed it, and stops when somebody takes care of them. Then as soon as they can crawl, they follow the big people everywhere, so that they are not left alone to be eaten by wild animals or anything. If a baby is alone, nature made it to be terrified, to cry really loudly and try to follow the big people, no matter what!

"And you, Hunter, tried holding Faith, carrying her, feeding her, and changing her. But it didn't work. The crying went on and on. When that happens, no matter how big their eyes are and how squishy their noses are, babies seem much more bad than good to their brothers who can't comfort them, right?"

"Right."

"So, I was bad, right?" said Faith, making a face and trying to sound impressively nasty. "I wasn't cute and squishy. I was a screaming monster."

"A poop machine!" said Hunter.

"No, honey, you weren't bad," said Toni, softly. "You couldn't be bad. You were a baby. A lonely little baby who was scared and hurting. With a lonely brother who was just as scared, and just as hurting as you were. You were two little kids who really, really needed parents to take care of you."

"That's right!" pronounced Helen. "You were MY kids, only nobody knew it yet! And my kids were good, not bad!"

"Uh, make that OUR kids, please," said Toni, her voice still soft.

Faith was feeling warm now, and sleepy in Toni's lap. It felt almost good, even though Toni was making it sound serious and not laughing about it the way Faith wanted them to. Toni really believed that Faith and Hunter had been sad, hurt, and alone back then. Toni was sad about it. Helen wanted to protect them. It was all strange; she and Hunter had never talked about it this way before.

Then Faith shook herself awake. What am I doing, in Toni's lap? she wondered. What about the Martins? Don't I love them anymore? And what if I get all comfy and then just have to leave again? I've got to be tougher than this! But it was like telling a drowning person not to hold onto the side of the pool, or a hungry person not to eat the donut. She needed that soft lap and those arms and kisses, just this once. Just this once, she told herself, and tomorrow, I'll be tough again.

Chapter 12: Faith Strikes Out

Faith was confused. She loved the Martins, and yet they had not kept her. Maybe they just didn't know how much she loved them, or how she would miss them. And now, she was starting to feel at home at the Greens. If she started to love the Greens, how would George and Ruby Martin ever know that she wanted them the most? And if they didn't know how much she needed them, they would never take her back, and the family she had with them would always be broken.

So time was running out, and Faith felt desperate to make her move. A plan was forming in her mind: she would run away, and Children's Services would ask the Martins to take her back.

But there were two problems. First, there was Hunter. How could she convince him to go, too? After what he said last night, about her being such a pain in the butt to look after, she thought his plans probably didn't include her as much as she always thought they had. Yet Hunter had always been there in her life, and she couldn't imagine being without him.

Second, there was Roscoe. She had to have Roscoe. But how to take Roscoe along, when Roscoe belonged to the Greens?

Faith remembered hearing something important from another foster child when she lived at the Martins. When you wanted to leave a place, the girl had told her, the best way to do it was to tell something on the foster parents that would make Children's Services move you. There were lots of things that you could tell: foster parents weren't sup-posed to hit, or call you names, or make you work too hard, or touch your privates, or go around half-naked (or naked!), or let you sleep with them, or do all kinds of kissy stuff in front of you. The kissy stuff was especially good for getting moved if the foster parents were both mums, or both dads; some social workers would get good and upset over kids seeing that! And the food had to be good and healthy, and they couldn't let you watch violent or sexy things on TV.

There was plenty of good stuff in there to tell—heck, some of the rules Helen and Toni had already broken, for real. Didn't they take her into bed with them after the nightmare? And she had seen them kiss and snuggle, and go around in pajamas. They sure made her work hard, stacking wood and cleaning up the floor. One day, after spilling her milk (an accident!) they had made her clean it all up, and it had taken over an hour. They made her keep going back until she had every single drop! And they did the same with her room—she had to keep trying until every single thing was put away, even if it took all day on a Saturday! So, there was plenty to tell, and most of it could be true.

But what about Hunter, and Roscoe? Hunter didn't have to cooperate. If she could really convince the social workers that the Greens couldn't be trusted, they would take Hunter away, too. And as long as they were taking both kids away, reasoned Faith, they might as well keep them together!

So that was it! She could get the social workers to take Hunter away from the Greens as well. And she could do the same with Roscoe— show the social workers that the Greens weren't taking care of him! She just had to make it really, really convincing. It would take more than a story to the teacher; she would have to look the part—a desperate run-away on her own. She had to plan ahead, carefully.

The Greens were late sleepers when they didn't have to get up early. On Saturdays, Faith and Hunter usually played in their pajamas until ten or eleven o'clock, when bleary-eyed Toni and Helen would emerge, grateful for the quiet time. Faith and Hunter were even allowed to fix their own breakfast while they waited for the adults to rise. Yes, thought Faith, Saturday will be the day.

Faith set her alarm clock on Friday night for 6 a.m., and hoped that it didn't wake anybody else but her. If it did, she would have to say that it was an accident, and wait for another day.

It worked. At 6 a.m., Faith was awake even before the alarm, which she turned off. She tiptoed into the adult's bathroom, looking for eye shadow and a pair of sharp scissors. First, she cut herself some crooked bangs. They looked awful. Next, she used the make-up to give herself two black eyes with green and purple 'bruises.' She took the scissors to a t-shirt, creating a tear from the hem to her armpit. Very nice, she thought. She pulled out the jeans that had fit her in the summer, but were now too short and too tight around the middle. For good measure, she poked a hole in each knee. Then she kneeled down to Roscoe, who was already at her heels, and offered him some kibbles while she snipped large clumps of the beautiful, silky fur away and put them in the toilet.

When she finished, she cleaned up, and put some clothes under her covers to look like a sleeping version of herself. She needed to be warm (it was a long walk on a rainy morning), but she didn't want to show up in her new winter coat, so she dressed in layers with a summer windbreaker on top. She slipped out the door, with Roscoe on the leash, before anyone else had awakened.

It was a long walk to Children's Services, but it wasn't hard to find the way. At first, Faith was afraid that Helen and Toni would find her before she got there, but she had gone out without permission now enough times that they would probably first just wait for her to come home, especially since she left her coat. They would think she'd be cold. The ancestors might find some sneaky way to alert them. Funny, how they could do that, even without showing themselves. But even the ancestors seemed to have slept in, and Faith and Roscoe made the long walk alone.

When they arrived, Faith walked up to the heavy front door and pulled. But the doors were locked! How could I be so stupid? thought Faith. Of course, they're closed on Saturday! Now she was getting cold; she really didn't have enough layers of clothing on to stay warm in the rain. Her runners were soaked. Roscoe looked up at her, and tilted his head to one side. "What do we do now, buddy?" she asked. Roscoe wagged his tail.

"Well, I guess it's the police station." Faith turned and began walking in the direction of the station, a kilometer or two away. To keep Roscoe from worrying, she started to talk.

"Roscoe, don't worry if they separate us for a while. I have a plan. See, the police will probably take you to the SPCA, but the SPCA won't allow the Greens to pick you up, because they will see that you aren't well taken care of there. Just wait for me a little while, until I can talk the Martins into coming to get you. First, I'll make them bring me to visit you every day, and I'll cry and cry to bring you with me. I won't even be faking it! You'll have other dogs to play with, and I'll bring you treats, I promise. I will be really, really good, better than I've ever been, except for crying all the time until they let me have you. Nobody can resist an eight-year-old who misses her dog, right?"

Roscoe wagged his tail, a little limply. It was raining now, hard and cold.

"This will work. The Martins will take us back. It will be okay."

Roscoe nudged her hand for a kibble.

"Yeah, I've got some. Here." Then, because she couldn't think of anything else to say, she hummed to Roscoe.

After a long, long time, they finally arrived, wet and bedraggled, at the police station.

"At least we're going to look like we really need help," said Faith.

"Can I help you?" asked the woman behind the plexiglass.

"Yes. I need to talk to your child protection officer, please." Faith tried to sound brave, spunky and sad, like "Annie" in a play she'd seen once.

"Just a minute. Please have a seat. And let me take the dog."

"No!" cried Faith, without even having to fake her alarm. This was not going well.

"He's m-m-my, best friend! I need him! We will both be really, really good. Please let him stay with me!"

"I can't take that chance, kiddo. Weird people come in through that door. Somebody might scare him, and make him bite."

"But he's on a leash! And he doesn't bite, except maybe to protect me. I go where he goes." Faith now sounded more certain, braver and stronger.

"Well, come with me, then. Both of you." The woman came out a side door, and led Faith and Roscoe down a hallway and into a small room. She closed the door.

Faith waited, and waited. She had to go to the bathroom. She could hear voices, but not make out what they were saying. Finally, she opened the door and walked back toward the big room where the woman sat, waiting on the phone.

"Can I go to the bathroom, please?" asked Faith.

"Over there," the woman pointed to a door coming right off the main office. "You can take the dog with you."

Faith went in. She looked in the mirror, and sighed. Her "bruises" didn't look so good now; they were streaking. She tried to do a repair job with paper towels. But when she got back to their little room, darn tears started rolling down her cheeks, probably messing it all up again. She left the door ajar, so she could hear.

"We have a report on a missing child with a dog," the woman was saying. "And I think they're in room A."

Faith jumped up, but, without a plan, sat down again. Heavy footsteps were coming down the hall.

"What's your name, kid?" asked the big police officer. Faith kept one eye on the gun at his side, but other than that, he didn't look mad or anything. He looked like the kind of dad every kid wanted, she thought. Strong, kind of good looking, a little bit bald in front.

"Faith Paley," she answered, defeated.

"Paley? Not Green?"

"Oh, yeah. Green. Paley is my real name, but the Greens adopted me so now I have their name."

"I see. So, you are new to the Greens?"

"Yes, sir." She was glad she remembered the 'sir' part.

Then she was remembering other things, too. She had been here before. Had she seen this man then? Was he there when she and Hunter were taken from home, back when Roxanne left and Roger was asleep on the couch and wouldn't wake up? Had he picked here up then, and walked out with her? Or was that a different cop? She only remembered the belt, the gun, and the strong arms picking her up. And Hunter, running and trying to hide, then crying and fighting. But she hadn't fought or anything, had she? She had just put up her arms and been carried out, right out of that house and to another. There had been a short time in the first home, where she ate and ate soup and peanut butter sandwiches and saltine crackers in milk. And then the Martins. And then the Greens, five years later.

"Um, I can't go back there, sir." She pulled her thoughts back to the present, and tried to remember her lines. She had rehearsed them in her head, all the way from home to Children's Services. She had to do this! "They are mean to me, and to Roscoe, too. They don't give me warm clothes, see? And they hit me. Helen punched me in the face, see? And Roscoe tried to run away, because they kept hitting us, and he got into thistles and they cut his hair away, see? And now he doesn't have enough fur, and he looks bad because they wouldn't even take him to a groomer. They can't take care of kids, sir, and they can't take care of dogs, either."They don't feed us enough, and it's mostly candy. And they kiss in front of us, all the time! And they are both women! And, sir, they make me sleep in their bed with them. And they walk around all the time in just their pajamas or their underwear. And, and …" she tried to remember more, but if she made it too complicated, she might forget and make mistakes later. "We need a new home."

There, it was done. Hope rose within her. Maybe the officer would take her home with him! Maybe he would remember her, and be sorry he didn't take her the first time! I'll bet he has a big house, she thought, and a wife who really likes kids. I bet he remembers me, and feels bad that things didn't work out. I bet he'd be a great dad. If the Martins really can't take us, then maybe these people will.'

"I'm officer Brentwood. You can call me Mike." He had that, warm, 'let's just get to know each other' tone, which she liked. She was suddenly really hungry, and wondered whether what they said was true, about policemen and donuts. She could really use a donut now. Or three.

"What's that on your face?" asked Mike the policeman.

"Bruises!" said Faith, looking tragic.

"Let me see," he said, and pulled out a cloth handkerchief.

"Don't touch me!" Faith shouted, caught by surprise. "It will, it will hurt too much!" There, would that hold him off? No, here he came, handkerchief in hand. He wiped at her "bruises", and the handkerchief turned green and purple. This was starting to not go so well.

"Uh huh. And did you give yourself the hair cut too? And the dog?"

"No," she answered, meekly.

"Listen, Faith," said Officer Mike. "The Greens are on their way here, with your brother. Don't you want to tell me before they get here why you needed to run away?"

"I told you! They are mean to me!"

"Well, maybe they are, sweetheart," he said, kindly. "But without real bruises, I have to let you go back with them, anyway. At least until next week. But I think that there is more going on here than you're telling me."

"Well," she thought fast. Was it time to bring out the Big Lie, the one that would surely get results? She could say that they touched her privates, couldn't she? Wouldn't that work, and who could say that they hadn't? Didn't police have to believe that one? One foster kid had told her that it worked so fast that she wouldn't even get in trouble—they'd find her a new home right away if they thought she was being sexually abused. She looked to Roscoe for courage. "They, um, they ..."

She looked at Roscoe and there, riding side-saddle, was Grandpa Green. The one ancestor she thought would not follow her. After all, he was Helen's dad, and no relation to her. No relation to her by blood, anyway. And he was a Reverend! It was like those cartoons with the devil on one shoulder, and an angel on the other, she thought. Only he didn't really look very angelic, or like a Reverend. He was just sitting there, looking at her with sad eyes, kind of like Roscoe. How could somebody be so old, and look so innocent? Like he just wanted her to come home.

Faith started crying in earnest now. This was a bad idea. The Martins wouldn't really take her; they didn't even live where they could have kids anymore. And Toni would cry, and Helen would put her arms around Toni and try to comfort her. And they would be so sad. She wanted them to be embarrassed and angry, but she couldn't picture it. They'd just be sad, like Grandpa Green. And then what? She'd move, and then? Move again. And then? Move again. She'd get bigger, and less cute. Nobody would want her after a while. Hunter didn't want her. Nobody knew where her father was. Grandma Lily was a drunk, and scared Faith. So did Roxanne, who would have some other scary man with her by now.

She could hear Toni and Helen arriving. "Where is she?""Is she here?"

"Can we see her?" the voices were urgent, worried.Faith listened. If they got angry and blew up, officer Mike would keep her. Faith half-wished that this would happen, and half-hoped that it would not. But neither of the mothers sounded angry; just worried. Faith gave up."Excuse me, Sir," she blubbered, her eyes downcast in embarrassment. Roscoe was pulling her out the door, barely containing himself in his excitement. His family was back together! She let him pull her out, and into the arms of Toni. Helen came around and embraced her from behind. Surrounded, she peeked out to see Hunter, his hand on his forehead, shaking his head as though to say, 'what put this into your crazy head?'

Now, Faith realized that she felt relieved after all. It was time to go home.

Chapter 13: The BS-ometer

Faith thought that Helen and Toni would be furious when they got home. She braced herself for a huge punishment and lots of yelling. But the storm didn't come. If she looked closely, she thought that Helen was working hard to contain her emotions. Her face was red, and she hung out mostly by herself until evening. She took her usual weekend nap, and shut herself into her office to do paperwork. Toni was left to handle Faith, and she did so matter-of-factly. They took Roscoe for a walk, and Toni wondered aloud why Faith had been so desperate to run away. Had she missed the Martins so much? Or was it about how hard it was to be at the Greens? Or to be adopted? Since Faith didn't feel much like talking, she let Toni wonder.

That evening, they all slept together in the living room, by the wood-stove. Toni snuggled close to Faith and played "this little piggy" with her toes, which made her laugh because it was silly. Helen wanted to play it with Hunter's toes, but he said, "no!" and pulled away his feet.

Hunter was acting strangely. When Helen pulled Hunter close, he leaned away, and when Toni tried to do the same, he glared at her and looked angry. Faith wondered why Hunter was acting angry at Helen, when it was she who had run away.

It was nice by the woodstove, though, and Roscoe slept between the children on the floor, where they could both reach out and pet him.

Faith didn't really want to tell Toni how she felt about running away, but on the trail of an emotion, Toni was like a dog with a bone. The next morning, the questions began in earnest.

"What feelings did you have when you left?"

"I don't know."

"Well, if you did know, what would you guess?" Faith might not be in a whole lot of trouble, but she began to wish that these were the kind of parents who punished and yelled, instead of this talking and thinking about everything! Yelling was over when it was over. Even hitting was over when it ended. But this thinking, and talking, and thinking— where would it lead?

Faith wondered why it had never occurred to her that Toni and Helen would feel really bad over what she did. Or had it? Did she want them to feel bad for all the times when they made her do chores when she didn't want to, or put on her coat, or wear what they said to wear, or eat what they said to eat? Was that it? Or had she just wanted to get away?

Anyway, she didn't want them to feel so bad anymore. Still, she had done it; she had gone to the police with a real whopper of a story, and, even though she didn't tell it in the end, it probably looked pretty bad to officer Mike. He must think I am a really, really bad kid, thought Faith. And, if he was the one who had taken her from Roxanne and Roger, what would he think of her now? That she didn't deserve a better home? That she was bad, and was going to end up like her parents, who lied, screamed and hit, and did drugs and left children to take care of themselves?

Toni kept trying to get Faith to talk about it, but she just didn't want to.

For now, they settled on a plan for consequences. First, Faith needed to get her hair cut to look nice again, and she needed to pay for that with her own saved allowance money. Second, she would, with Helen's help, make a coat for Roscoe, to hide the gaps and keep him warm and dry until his own fur grew out again. Third, they would no longer be allowed to take care of themselves on Saturday mornings; one of the mums would have to get up with them to supervise. Finally, Faith was to write a paragraph about how she decided to run away, and what her plan had been.

Faith decided to start right away, to get this over with. She sat in her room, with Hunter there reading a book, and tried to think of a worthy story that she could use.

"How about this," she tried out, "I was trying to groom Roscoe, and made some mistakes. Then, I wanted to take him for a walk, but we got lost, and the police picked us up in their car."

"Whoo boy!" came from the dresser-top. Sure enough, the committee of ancestors had assembled. I should have expected this, she thought. "That's a whopper! All the way to fifty!" Uncle Pete was staring at something about the size of the palm of his hand that looked like a compass. The others bent in close to see.

"What is that?" asked Hunter, moving in to have a look. The compass was marked off in sixty increments around the circle, like minutes on a clock. It had just one "hand", though, a single needle that was pointing to the "50" mark. The face of the "clock", or compass, whichever it was, was divided like a pie into six, 10-point segments, and each had a label. One to 10 was "Reasonably Historical", 10 to 20 was "A bit fuzzy on the details", 20 to 30 was "Literary License", 30 to 40 was "Stretching Credibility", 40 to 50 was "Deliberate Deception", and 50 to 60 was "Real Whoppers".

"It's a Bullshit Detector," replied Uncle Pete.

"Come on, Uncle Pete, you know that you are not supposed to swear around us. We are children!" Faith was relieved to have someone present whose behaviour was sometimes possibly worse than her own. Uncle Pete could always be relied upon for a good distraction.

"Okay, okay, it's a BS-ometer, then. Tells lies from truth.""

"Where did you get it?" asked Hunter, and then felt foolish. Where did ghosts get things? All of their possessions had that half-see-through look that they themselves had. Obviously, he didn't get it at the hardware store.

"Oh, sometimes we just find things in our pockets. Been carrying it around a long time, now, and I must say it's been much more interesting to me since movin' in here."

"Are you saying we BS a lot?"

"Well, all I'm sayin' is that I've had to ditch my digital one and go back to this—the digital one had an alarm beep that set my nerves on edge. I haven't been so jittery since I quit drinkin' in 1918! This one is quiet."

"So, you don't believe me, then." said Faith.

"Not for a minute."

"Then what am I going to say?"

"Try the truth," suggested Grandpa Green, his innocent eyes wide and expectant.

Faith sat down on the floor, defeated. Really, Grandpa Green could be so … so

… inexperienced. For somebody who lived to be an old man, how could he go around thinking that people just spilled the truth about things like this? Had he never needed to keep anything private in his long life?

"Didn't you ever have to lie, Grandpa?" she asked.

"Have to? I don't think so. Choose to? A few times; every child does," he replied. "But by the time I'd been to Bible School I guess I was afraid to tell lies, for fear of what God would do when he heard me!"

"Are you kidding me?" asked Hunter. "You thought God would punish you, just for lying?"

"Well, remember, I was just a little kid. I didn't understand God very well then. Some people still think God is up there, keeping a list of bad deeds to punish us over someday. But God's not like that, really. Once you know God's love, you just want to behave—that's the way it works."

"Yes, but what about lying?" Faith didn't want to get Grandpa Green going on religion just now. She was still hoping for some juicy confession from Uncle Pete. "Didn't any of you lie?"

"Whoo boy! Lie? Why do you think they gave me this thing after my death? Hopin' I'd learn to tell the truth from lies in the afterlife, I suppose. I sure told my share of whoppers before I died, let me tell you!"

"Sometimes, a person has no choice but to lie, or at least hide things," said Oma Mika, her accent thick today and her eyes looking far into the past.

"Tell us, Oma. Who were you, and why did you lie in life?" asked Faith, whose curiosity was real. This Oma looked so much like Toni that Faith wanted to know her.

"Well, it was a long time ago; longer than any of these others. When I was a little girl my family lived in a village in Russia. We didn't own the land, and many people were being forced to move in those days. My father, he was a smart man who read. One day, in the attic, I found a book among the dried onions and bunches of herbs. I never did know what it was; my father threw it into the fire. He told me that I must never, ever tell anyone that I had seen it, or he would have to go far, far away and I would never see him again. It might have been something about the church, or about the Tsar; I do not know. That was when I first understood that there were secrets in life that could kill, and that lying was necessary when dealing with the world.

"Later, I had a son, Ivan. I was very young, and not married so we moved to Königsberg and pretended that Ivan was my little brother. When he was just sixteen, he got involved in the worker's union. I could not keep him safe, and as long as he stayed at home, we were all in danger. So he had to go. It was like in the fairy tales, where the sons go 'off to seek their fortune'; we said our goodbyes and did not see him again …"

"What happened to him?" asked Faith, who, though she didn't understand all of the story, felt the sadness of Oma in its telling.

"He went west, to Berlin, and studied there. Berlin. He was a scholar of the working people! Finally, he was murdered by the Nazis in a concentration camp for political prisoners. They didn't like his ideas any more than the Russian Tsars had liked the ideas of his grandfather.

"But I married and had another child, Hannah. She was Antonia's grandmother.

"All things were dangerous then! I became a widow at 30. I learned to deliver babies and to find and prepare the plants that made medicine in those days. I became a healer, and this was a useful trade to have. When the Great War came too close, we had to move on. But the plants were similar, and mothers and babies are the same everywhere. I had plenty of work."I had a friend, Anya. She was having a baby, which was too early and so it died. Afterward, she stayed with me. She was good to little Hannah, and I came to love and depend upon her in every way. She was like the Virgin Mary, whose shrine I had sought out in every church and cathedral since my childhood. I apologize, Reverend Green, if this shocks you, but to me, God could not be a man."

"Hey!" said Hunter, "You can't say that! It's 'God the Father,' right Grandpa?"

"Hunter," said Grandpa Green gently, "God is love. Oma is right, and so are you. If you need God to be your father, he is. And if you need him to be a mother, well, she's that too. God is also your brother and your sister—just see if you can spot him in the faces of people you know."

Oma Mika continued, "Yes, well, I did see God in my Anya's face, every morning and every night. And in my Hannah. Just like Toni and Helen, your mamas. We had to keep things simple, so we told people we were sisters.

"So that was another lie—how many am I up to? My father's reading, my little brother who was my son, his politics and where he went, and finally my friend who became my sister. That should be enough to get me a good score on that BS-ometer, Uncle Pete.

"But it was so lonely, living with those lies! I had to be so careful. With everyone that I met, no matter how friendly they were, I thought, 'you don't know me at all'. If they had known me, really known me, would they have turned me in? And I didn't really know anyone in return! Only Anya and Hannah. The Tsar, the Church, the Revolutionists, Stalin, the Nazis—they made liars out of everyone. I was so happy to know that my great, great granddaughter had come to Canada, where she did not have to lie in order to live. It is a great freedom to be able to tell the truth about who you are, where you came from, and what you believe in."

"Well, I guess so," said Hunter, "but does it really count as a lie if you have to say it, or maybe somebody will get killed? I mean, it's not like when Faith lies to get out of trouble."

"Or when you lie to impress people!" Faith retorted.

"I do not!"

"Yes, you do."

"Oh, this thing gits quite a workout 'roun here," said Uncle Pete, holding up the BS-ometer. "And yer' both right, lyin' to save a life ain't the same as lyin' to get out of trouble or to impress people. But ya' have to be careful about lyin'. It's an easy habit ta git, and a tough one ta break."

"Why break it?" asked Hunter, who often found lying easier than telling the truth. Neither he nor Faith could see what the big problem was, other than getting caught in lies seemed to get them into "consequences" with Helen, who would make them write lines like, "Lies break trust" when she caught them.

"Well, if you were payin' attention, you'd know that lyin' makes ya lonely. Everybody needs somebody who knows the truth about 'em, and loves 'em anyway," stated Uncle Pete. "Also, if you're gonna live in a family, you hafta follow the family rules. And rule number one is, 'Don't lie to yer mothers.'"

"What do you know about family rules?" asked Nana Rose. "You were a bachelor all your life, and an ornery one at that."

"Well, that's what makes me the expert! I'm the only one here who knows what not livin' in a family is like, and it's not a good trade for the privilege of lyin' whenever ya want to. A family can't work very well if people don't tell the truth ta each other. Ya gotta have truth between people. You can avoid it, and be alone in life, but that ain't no picnic, I'm tellin' ya."

"But sometimes I like to lie," admitted Hunter. "It's like having something private of my own; why should I let other people know what's in my head? I know what is true and what is false, but they don't need to, do they?"

"Oh, ay, like yer brain is your private little room," nodded Pete. "I remember that feelin'. It's the other side of the loneliness your Oma had. Some of us don't mind bein' our own company alone, and some of us think the company of others is too dangerous to share—even in our own families. If those people know the truth about ya, ay, well, they won't love ya, you think."But if they don't know all about ya, then how can they love all about ya? Ya think they can love that cardboard mask person that you hold in front of yourself? Think nobody will notice that it's thin and fake-lookin'? Well, that's a pretty hard thing to love! So, there ya are—all alone no matter how ya look at it!"Nope, there's some people you oughtta give a chance to know yer truths, and to love ya'. Give'em a chance, and people like Toni and Helen usually come through, and surprise ya."

"How do you know they will?" asked Faith.

"Ya keep yer eyes open! Watch for the signs! How do they talk to each other? Do they take care o' Roscoe? Do they kick him out when he's a bad boy? No! Do they pay their bills, take care of their house, look after their friends? Never rest on blind faith, my boy but learn what a good bed looks like!"

"What are the other family rules? Who wrote them?" asked Faith.

"Oh, we've been teaching ya. There's 'don't abandon people', and 'stick close together', 'stand up fer each other', and 'touch each other every day,' for instance. And 'help each other out', and ..."

"Wait!" Hunter had jumped up, "What's that touch thing? That's just kind of creepy! Why are Toni and Helen always doing that—they like, rub my hair and put their arms around me and stuff. Toni even wanted me to hold hands! They sneak up out of nowhere and hug me from behind. Why is that in the rules?"

"That, my boy, is for another day. Right now, I think we need to help Faith with her paragraph assignment. She needs help finding the words, right lassie?"

"Yes, okay. Please."

Dear Toni and Helen,

I am sorry that I tried to run away with Roscoe. I had a plan for getting us back to the Martins. And I made Roscoe look like nobody took care of him so he could come with me. oh, and I also made me look like nobody took care of me and like I had black eyes.

I'm probably going to be bad some more times, but I will try to be good. I think maybe I want to live with you.

Faith.

PS. I was going to tell a bad lie about you, but I didn't. I'm glad.

Chapter 14: That Touch Thing

If there was one thing about families that Hunter didn't. understand, it was that touching thing. Parents always wanted to hug, to touch your hair, to rub your back, even to hold you hand. To Hunter, that was for babies. And maybe girls. But he noticed that men did not have to do it, and he didn't want to do it, either.

One day, he was working on his bicycle with Uncle Pete, who was good at machines, and he decided to bring it up. "Uncle Pete, did you like being touched when you were alive?"

"Well, just how do you mean it, 'touched'? Like, 'I'm pesterin' you' touching? Where other kids put their fingers on your desk, or on your stuff, or on your skin like they own it? Or, like, 'I'm your parent and you belong to me so you will do whatever I say,' touch? Or like, 'I'm going to be nice to you and then you will touch my privates' touch? Can't say I ever liked any of those, myself."

"I guess not! Touch is just nasty!" agreed Hunter. "Why would anybody like it? It's gross! But Toni and Helen are all touchy, all the time! They won't leave me alone, even though I tell them I don't like it. Like, with the hair. They want to touch my hair and stuff, and Helen gets mad at me when I don't wash my hair because then she says that she doesn't want to touch it, and I just think, 'good! It's my hair!'"

"Ah, yes. I believe that's called 'affection.' To them, it's not pesterin'. That's a real problem," sighed Uncle Pete. "I'd better call the committee together. Me, I never really did get the touch thing—I think I died too young to figger it out."

"No! At least, don't call all of them. Maybe Grandpa Green."

"Grandpa Green? He was the biggest, sloppiest, touching-est one of all of us! Are you kiddin' me? He used to sit right up front of his church with three, four, five tiny little kids on his lap at once! Puttin' their fingers on his pipe, feelin' his whiskers! What's he gonna know about touch?"

"Well, maybe if he liked touch, he can tell me why Helen likes it so much. And maybe he can help me know how to get out of it without hurting her feelings. She says it makes her sad when I don't want to be touched."

"So, you're gettin' to like Helen, eh?"

"She's just easier than Toni, that's all. Not quite so huggy, and she lets you get by sometimes without having to find the words for every single thing. I don't want to hurt her feelings, is all."

"Yeah, I see that. She's also the one that has to hold her temper back! The words that she doesn't say would fill this whole backyard, and most of it would be blue!"

"Blue?"

"Swear words!"

"Really? Helen swears?"

"Not so much since you came along, but the Reverend Green says she used to love to swear! Said she learned it in college. Guess she had to rebel a little bit, bein' the Reverend's daughter." Uncle Pete's eyes sparkled and he winked at Hunter.

"Well, maybe you're right. We ought to have somebody here who liked touch when he was alive. Some ghosts really miss it, and the Reverend is one of them. Maybe he can explain what we're missin.'"

And there was Grandpa Green, looking silly on his small sitting stool, which he overflowed considerably.

Grandpa Green favored small stools or his wingback chair, and not much in between. He loved reading his books in the wingback chair, he said, or thinking with his pipe, or writing sermons. But he also liked to be close to the ground, where the children hung out and where he could watch small things, like the ground squirrel that lived in his yard back on the prairies. Bugs, he said were full of drama; whole empires of ants once came and went in the history of his front lawn. Helen told Hunter that her father loved the hymn "This is my Father's world." It used to amaze her, as a little girl in church, that there were songs in the hymnal about her dad. But she eventually figured out that they meant God. To Grandpa Green, she said, the words "the birds their carols raise, the morning light, the lily white declare their maker's praise" were true every day. Hunter wasn't sure he understood the words yet, but the poetry had to do with why Grandpa Green liked sitting close to the ground.

Grandpa Green looked up from studying the bugs, and seemed surprised to find himself among company. "Oh, hello, Hunter! Pete! Have I been summoned?"

"Looks like it, Rev!" said Uncle Pete with a smile. The two of them were a funny pair, thought Hunter. Grandpa Green was fat, educated, and loved scripture. Uncle Pete was skinny, skeptical, and didn't school past grade four.

Grandpa Green's life had been good, he said, and Hunter thought it sounded very good indeed. Even when Grandpa was a little boy his family had not gone hungry or without a home and clothing. Then he met Grandma Green and they had Helen, Aunt Harriet, and the "baby", Uncle Hugh, who nowadays drove a big rig for a living, and, at forty, still played in a rock 'n' roll band. Small towns, bare feet, adventures on bicycles and supper on the table when the streetlights went on; these were the things that Helen loved to tell about. Of course, there was lots of going to church, but Hunter didn't think he'd have minded that too much; he actually liked how peaceful it was at church. To Hunter, Grandpa Green's life seemed like a life made in heaven, or on TV. Nobody really lived that way, he thought. Except Helen, when she was small. Before she learned to swear.

Uncle Pete's life had been short and hard. Sometimes he lived with his mother in a tiny shack without much heat, where food was scarce and he was lonely when she went out to work for the better-off women in town. When his mother was ill, or just too poor to keep him, or wanted somebody to make him go to school, she would allow her sister to come and get him and he'd go live with the cousins, where he was "almost like one of the family" except that he wasn't.

The cousins stuck together against Pete, and blamed him for anything that got broken or stolen or just misplaced. He had to wear their out-grown clothes, which were usually too small for him, too. They played tricks on him and threatened him if he told. His aunt made everyone promise to look after "poor little Pete," but they didn't, of course. They didn't like having to share what they had, Pete now understood, because nobody had very much.

So Pete had left as early as he could. He worked the boats, fishing with whoever would have him until he was seventeen, then he signed up to go to the Great War, World War I. "It wasn't so great, after all," he told Hunter. "Thought I'd see the world! Maybe fly one of them air-o-planes. Oh, what a wonder they was! Whoo-ee! I'd have given any-thing. But they give me a test to see how smart I was, and I guess a boy without much schoolin' weren't too smart, so they sent me to the front. I managed to stay alive for nearly two years, before a shell got me. Nothin' left o' me; not even a body to send back home. Which was no great tragedy, since I can't say my body was much of a specimen. But I wish I'd have seen more of the world. I learned to read in them trenches; there wasn't much else to do there, and I liked it all right. The Bible was puzzlin', but my buddy Arthur came up with Treasure Island, and that was fine stuff, I'm a-telling you!"

And now, here they were, side by side, like old friends. Pete liked to tease "the Reverend" a bit about his good fortune, and of course there was envy under the tease.

But Grandpa Green never seemed to mind, and he listened to Pete's stories and point of view as though it was Pete who told the sermons, and it was Grandpa's time to learn. To Grandpa Green, Pete's story was like one of the adventures he used to read as a child, only with all of the sadness and hard feelings still there to understand. To Pete, Grandpa Green's life was good enough to make him almost believe, and to really want to believe, the good things about God that had escaped his notice during his own short time among the living.

And now, Grandpa Green was talking about touch as though it were one of those good things.

"Did you know," he began, "that the sense of touch is the very first one we have as a baby? It's the only sense that we are born with already perfect, ready to go. Oh, the ears work pretty well, too, once they slurp the gunk out of them. But touch, that's superb. And all the scientists in the world still don't understand exactly how it works! There are little organs in the skin ..."

"Organs? Like church organs?" asked Pete.

"No, not like that. They don't make music, exactly. Some of them look like tiny onions, with layers. They detect pressure on the skin. Others detect heat, or pain, or movement like a light, stroking touch. Itching and tickling are mysteries—nobody knows how they work, but they seem to involve all of the sensors in the skin.

"And babies have an amazing touch sense. It goes along with their hearing, and also their sense for how they are being held—like, sideways or upside down or, hopefully, calmly and close, like this" and he demonstrated a cradling hold with a towel that he had produced out of nowhere—"or this", and he held the 'baby' to his shoulder—"or even this, the football hold!" and he held the "baby" face down in the crook of his arm.

"When the baby hears the mama or papa's voice, and feels all snug like this, then it feels good. The baby learns to love its parents that way. Touch is part of how family love begins for babies."

Hunter had about a million questions. "But what if people hold the baby the wrong way, like upside-down or something? What if they drop it? Or what if, just goofing around, they throw it? Babies don't really feel stuff like that, do they? "

"That would be a bad thing. Yes, what I'm telling you is that babies feel everything!"

"Even a pinch?"

"Yes"

"Even a needle?"

"Yes."

"But I heard that babies get a needle in their foot, right after they are born! Why would doctors do that if babies feel pain?" asked Hunter, still not quite believing.

"Because they are taking a blood sample to see whether the baby has an illness that they need to know about right away so they can treat it. They put eye drops in, too, that probably sting, but it's to prevent a kind of blindness that can happen. So, in the hospital, painful things do happen to babies. Nowadays they give the baby right to its mother for comfort after those things. And she soothes the baby with touch."

"But babies don't remember any of that," said Hunter.

"Not as memories," explained Grandpa Green, "But if the hospital is a painful place, then they may still feel that way about hospitals many years later, and not know why. Their feelings remember, even if the story part of their brain doesn't. Some people call this a 'body memory.'"

"Wow. Okay, go on. So, babies like touch. Why don't Uncle Pete and I?"

"Well, for most babies, it works really well. They get held and touched nicely, and that calms them down and makes them happy. Then, because they go from sad to happy, they come to think of 'parents', 'touch', and 'happy' all together. Anything that even reminds them of their parents can make them feel better, especially if something bad, like getting a needle or being pinched, happens to them. Little by little, comfort by comfort, babies learn how to love and be loved, and how to feel comforted by love. They learn to look to their mamas and papas for comfort. Then, even when they're big and crawling around, or walking around, or riding tricycles or bikes or in cars, they still, their whole lives, think of their parents and remember how that loving touch, and holding, felt. It's called 'attachment', and it means the feeling you have for the person who makes you feel better."

"Does that mean that me and Pete are not attached to anybody?" asked Hunter, feeling a little sad and scared.

"Well, I guess it means you aren't really attached in a secure way to anybody. And that's not so surprising. You didn't have that constant source of comfort when you were little, and, when you did have it, it wasn't safe enough or around long enough for you to get the feelings lodged really strongly within you.

"Also, the memory of good touch is fragile," Grandpa Green went on. "It's easily hurt and changed. If something hurts you by touch, your body remembers it and wants to avoid that thing forever."

"Like when Roxanne's boyfriend Denis pushed Faith's face into the carpet, and hit me on the back?"

"Yes, that would certainly stop your body's desire to be touched."

"And, like, sometimes people cozy all up to kids, and it feels like they must really like you, but it turns out they want something from you, like your lunch money or your bike, or maybe even to have sex with you! I hate that!" Hunter shivered unexpectedly.

"So, babies like touch because, if nobody messes it up by bein' real mean to 'em, it makes 'em feel good. And if somebody messes that up, we stop likin' it," summed up Uncle Pete. "But what about this kid's mothers? Why are they so fired up on touch?"

"Yeah?" asked Hunter. "I don't ask for it."

"Well, touch feels good both ways. Parents are just made that way, I guess; if babies are made to like touch, then parents have to like touching their children. Otherwise, it wouldn't work out so well, would it? Touching their children makes parents feel like they are a real family. It's like a little reward that they get for all the things that they sacrifice for you, and the ways they take care of you."

"So, do I have to let them touch me?" asked Hunter.

"Only if you don't want them to be unhappy," replied Grandpa Green.

"Even when I'm a teenager?"

"Yes, even when you're an adult."

Hunter thought about this. "Will it always feel so strange and gross?" he asked, finally. "I really do hate it."

Uncle Pete looked at him and winked. "Oh, now, wait 'til you have a girlfriend! Or a wife, even! And don't ya want to cuddle babies of your own? I never got ta do that! And isn't there any little part of ya in there that likes it?"

"No, not really. Except for the dogs—I like to cuddle the dogs. But they aren't people; they aren't going to hurt me. Sure, I'd like a girlfriend, but I don't think I want to do the kissing and everything. Just, you know, maybe hold hands."

Grandpa Green took over. "It gets easier with practice. It's like having a fear of something, like going across bridges or riding a horse. The longer you avoid it, the stronger the urge to avoid it becomes. If you keep turning and pulling away from little touches like a head rub or a hug, your body doesn't learn anything new; it stays with the 'yuk' feeling. But if you always avoided, say, horseback riding, you never know what you might be missing. And most people find touch to be wonderful! Just the thing to make life richer and happier. So it's worth it to try."

"You could start with something easy. Is there any part of you that feels okay to touch, or any kind of touch that isn't so bad?"

"Well," said Hunter, "I don't mind when Toni massages my feet. It's okay."

"Then ask her to massage your feet. She'll be so surprised! And you can stay in charge, because you are the one that asked. Just make sure they are clean and smell good!" said Grandpa Green.

Pete liked this idea. "It could be kind of her reward for fixin' ya a nice dinner. I know ya like the food at the Greens! You eat like a bear gettin' fat for the winter!"

Hunter smiled. Yes, he did like the food at the Greens, and there was always plenty of it. He could practically feel himself growing taller.

"Then, if I let her massage my feet, how will that help with the hugs?" he asked.

"Just give it time," said Grandpa Green, "and don't shrink away. If you can take a football tackle, you can take a hug."

"And what if they do something that hurts me, or feels terrible?"

"Speak out!" replied Grandpa Green. "You teach them what works. If you like massage that just runs the fingers gently across the skin, you can say that. Or if you like massage that is slow and deep into your muscles, you can say that. Or you can say,'more of that, please', when they get it just right. Didn't you ever need somebody to scratch your back when it itched?"

"Yeah."

"And did you tell them to go a little higher, or a little lower, or over to the left or the right?" asked Grandpa Green.

"Yeah," Hunter smiled a little again.

"Well, there ya go!" cried Uncle Pete. "You teach 'em! They teach you ta accept it, and you teach 'em ta get it right!"

"Exactly!" said Grandpa Green. "And here's the deal. I'll keep teaching you football, if you let Toni or Helen give you a good touch—a cuddle, or a back rub, or a shoulder rub, or fingers through your hair; something safe and good—every day. For now, I'll accept once a day, but by next month, I want to see it increase to twice a day! I don't want my grandson to be able to dish out and accept tackles if he can't also pick up a baby!"

"Well, if you put it that way," said Hunter, "I guess I have to do it."

"You won't be sorry," said Uncle Pete. "Yer a lucky boy. I was almost part of the family; yer a real son to these people."

"Yeah. Isn't it nuts?" asked Hunter. "Two women, just going along, minding their own business, and they say, 'let's get some kids!' Sometimes, I feel like I landed on a strange planet or something."

Grandpa Green and Uncle Pete looked at each other, then back at Hunter.

"Get used to it!" they said together.

Chapter 15: Hunter On His Own?

Whenever he could, Hunter went to the library. He really did have homework to do there, but it also gave him a chance to check for messages from his father on Facepage. There weren't many, but Hunter could go to his father's profile and see pictures. There were his cousins, his grandparents, his aunt, and his father's cat. There were things that might be there to attract a girlfriend; Gary's marital status was marked "single". But no pictures, and no mention of Hunter appeared there. Ever. Once he had checked for anything new, Hunter would settle down and work on his assignment. Today, it was researching Vincent Van Gogh. Hunter felt a bit like Vincent himself, he thought. He was in a melancholy mood.

That's a good word, thought Hunter, Melancholy. Not just sad. More lonely sounding, and aloof. I think I'll use it in my homework.

"Hey, Hunter! My man!" Hunter turned around to see a tall young man in a baseball cap and leather jacket. "What's up, man? Do you remember me? I'm Nathan."

"Nathan? From the Martins?" If Hunter looked closely, he could just make out the features of a boy he had known three years ago at George and Ruby's house. It was hard, because Nathan had changed a lot. He was taller by about a foot, and thinner as well. His once shoulder-length hair was cropped short under his cap. His face was more of a square shape now that it was thinner and his cheeks had nearly disappeared.

"What are you doing here?" asked Hunter, and then felt silly. Why shouldn't Nathan be here? It was a public library. Hunter had always felt a bit shy around Nathan, probably because Nathan was older than him, stronger and able to do things that Hunter couldn't. How old had he been, wondered Hunter, when he lived at the Martins? Nathan hadn't been there for more than a couple of months, but Hunter had loved having a "big brother" during that time. Nathan had introduced him to heavy metal music, car racing games on the computer, and Marvel Comics. Once, Nathan had offered him a cigarette, although Hunter had been only eight years old at the time! Hunter had declined, but he couldn't help wondering what it would be like, smoking with Nathan. Now he wondered what else Nathan might smoke, and whether he was still in school.

"I mean, how old are you now? Are you in foster care still? Do you, ah, go to high school?"

"Nope," replied Nathan. "Didn't finish. And, ah, no, I'm not in foster care anymore. I live in an apartment with my girlfriend. And I'm seventeen."

"Cool." Hunter was indeed impressed, although maybe not so much by Nathan's not being in school. "Do you have a job?"

"Yeah, I work for a construction company. Mainly I hang drywall. Sometimes I do roofing. Depends. What about you?"

"Um, I'm in school still. I'm ... thirteen," Hunter stretched the truth just a little bit. No more than a thirty on Uncle Pete's BS-ometer, he thought. "I go to Forest Park Middle School. Faith is in elementary school still."

"Well, I gotta go," said Nathan, "but why don't you stop over some time? We just live a block from here. I'm off for a few weeks; it's not building season. Here, I'll write it down for you." Nathan picked up one of the small papers by the computer and wrote down his address and phone number for Hunter, who tucked the paper into his jeans pocket.

The more he thought about it, the more Hunter did want to stop by Nathan's apartment, to see how he lived. I bet I can get some good pointers on how to get out on my own earlier, he thought. Heck, maybe Nathan and I could even share an apartment sometime. So the following day, he pressed Toni and Helen to allow him to go to the library from after school until supper time. From the library, he called Nathan's number.

"Hi, it's Hunter."

"Hey, little man! How's it goin'?"

"Good! I'm at the library, and I wondered if this was a good time to stop by."

"Sure, just watching TV. Skippin' out on your homework? C'mon over. The entrance is on the side of the house, under the carport."

Hunter found the house, and went around to the side, where he found the door to a basement apartment. He knocked, and Nathan answered.

The apartment looked like one room, really. It had small, high windows, and the walls looked like they had once been white. Maybe it was the orange shag wall-to-wall carpeting that smelled bad, thought Hunter. Something certainly did. A curtain hung over a doorway, perhaps hiding the bathroom. There was a small kitchen in one corner, a double mattress on the floor in the other. In between were a table with two mismatched chairs, a flowered couch that had seen better days, a stained and rickety coffee table, and some shelves made out of concrete blocks and boards, with a stereo, a TV, and some CDs and DVDs on them. There was a gaming console on the coffee table, and everywhere were dirty cups, plates, bowls and spoons. Some clothes lay in a pile next to the unmade bed; others spilled out of some cardboard boxes in the corner. Nathan is a slob! thought Hunter.

Nathan's cell phone rang just as he ushered Hunter in. "Come on in, Buddy," he motioned with one hand, the other holding his cell phone to his ear. "Yeah, my man! Got it! Be by about seven o'clock? Okay. Yep. No problem. Gotta go—see ya then." His attention came back to Hunter. "How's it hangin', little bro?"

"Uh, good!" said Hunter. "So, this is your place, eh? Where's your girlfriend?"

"Who, Julie? She's down at City Center, workin' on her GED."

"What's that?"

"Her high school equivalency. She wants to go to college, study for her Animal Care Aid. She likes animals."

Then Hunter noticed the aquarium beside the wall. "Hey! Nice lizard! It's a Bearded Dragon, isn't? I always wanted one of those!"

"Come here, little guy," said Nathan, as he reached in and picked up the large, lazy lizard and put it on his shoulder. "You like him, huh? Name's Lizardo. Not very original, I guess. But look, he's really cool! He watches TV with me and everything. Hey, you hungry?"

"No. Just ate, really." said Hunter, whose usually strong appetite had mysteriously disappeared in the apartment.

"Want to smoke some weed, then?" asked Nathan. "I got plenty. I can sell you some any time—just come to me. Best stuff, local, BC Weed. Organic, nothing cut in. I used to have my own plants, but the landlord won't allow no hydroponics. Lights and shit, you know, for growing."

"Uh, no thanks. I don't smoke yet. I'm just eleven," said Hunter. Then he remembered that he had told Nathan he was thirteen, and he wanted to melt right into the orange shag.

"How about a video game?"

"Yeah! sure!" Hunter sat on the edge of the flowered couch. "Hey, a Z-Box Infinity! Cool! What are you playing?"

"Vice Squad Quad," said Nathan. "Here, have you played it before?"

"No—how's it go?"

"You're this guy. You try to keep away from the cops, see, they look like this. And you have to knock off the rival gang members before they get you. You have to pick up your package and deliver it to the dropoff spot, then get another assignment."

"Okay, and how do I get one of those cars?"

"Those are armoured vehicles. You get a regular car at 1000 points, and an armoured one at 10,000."

"Hey, what's that girl doing?"

"Oh, never mind those. Here, we'll put her in the dumpster. Two hundred points! Yay!"

Gunfire erupted on the screen, and Hunter had to move his avatar fast around corners and down lanes. This was an exciting game! Although, he thought, it was a little bit violent. Time slipped by, and Hunter got a car, then an armoured vehicle by earning 10,000 points. He had shot more than 50 bad guys and six cops, and dumped two more of the strange girls in short dresses into dumpsters. A third one seemed to careen off his car as he sped off. Several times Nathan answered his cell phone with the same abrupt style and conversation Hunter had overheard when he came in.

Finally, the cell phone rang, and Nathan said, "Oh, hi Mum." Hunter looked up to see the stove clock indicate 5:30. Aargh!, he thought, I've been here nearly two hours! I'm going to be in trouble at home!'

Then he noticed that Nathan was no longer the smooth, cheery person he had been a few minutes ago. Something important was happening on the phone.

"What?" Nathan's voice rose in pitch, "They're coming here? No way! Jeez, oh, f**k!" He was pacing back and forth. "Why did you tell them where the f**k I was? What do you mean you didn't know? They're gonna f**k'n kill me! Oh, sh*t!"

Hunter hadn't heard "the f-word" so many times, in so many parts of speech, in years.

> Nathan turned off the phone, grabbed Hunter by the arm, and
> yelled, "Quick, get the f**k out of here! Get going! You can't
> stay here!" Hunter picked up his coat and backpack and scurried
> out the door, Nathan behind him. "Get to the library! Go!"

The two boys ran to the library. Nathan, who had left without a coat, kept looking over his shoulder. When they arrived, out of breath, Hunter could hardly wait to call home for a ride.

He didn't need to call; Helen was waiting for him, her arms crossed and one foot tapping.

"Where have you been?" she asked. Hunter groaned. All these weeks of good behaviour, of outshining Faith, and now he was in big trouble. And Nathan, well, it looked like Nathan was in even worse trouble somehow.

Chapter 16: Thinking it Over

After supper, Hunter went to his room to figure things out. He was, of course, barred from going to the library alone, and he had a writing assignment from "the mums"—explain where he had gone, and why. But, to his relief, there hadn't been much yelling. Hunter noticed that Helen was working hard to control her temper, just as Grandpa Green had said. But that hadn't stopped her from giving him a stern talking to in the car.

"I've been worried sick about you! How could you take advantage of my trust this way? I shouldn't have let you go there alone. I should have known it was too much responsibility. Still, I thought you could handle it! I thought I could trust you! Jeez, why did you have to prove me wrong?" Helen hit the steering wheel with her open hand.

Hunter had sat quietly, looking out the window. How could he tell her what he had seen and heard at Nathan's, or why he had gone?

And to think that just a few hours ago, he had daydreamed about moving out at sixteen to live with Nathan. Now, he knew better. Nathan was selling marijuana. Was that why he had invited him over? To get a customer? And what else was Nathan into? Was he involved with other drugs? Who was coming to get him, and why?

The phone call had come from Nathan's mother. Was she into the drug business, too? Was that why Nathan had been in foster care?

Hunter wondered how it would end for Nathan. Would he want to study and do something different, like his girlfriend Julie? Would he make his living building houses, like he said he did? Or was his real job selling drugs?

At home, in his room, Hunter just looked at the blank paper in front of him. He went over all that had happened again in his mind. Nathan was selling drugs. Why didn't he go to school anymore? Julie was finishing her high school and maybe going to college.

Then Hunter felt a heaviness in the pit of his stomach, like a rock dropping. Where was Julie? What if she had come home, just as the bad people came?

Was she somewhere safe?

Hunter didn't want to live like Nathan. He didn't want a basement suite that smelled bad, or a career running from angry drug dealers. He didn't want to be stuck with his mother's drug habit, or trying to protect her from mean guys. He wanted to go to college, to play football, to be somebody important, like a teacher or a coach. He wouldn't mind building houses, but only if that's what he really did; not dealing drugs in the rainy season. He wondered whether Nathan's life was unusual for foster kids who stayed in the system. Probably not, he thought. It's going to be easier getting started in life with Toni and Helen helping me. "Good thinkin'!" said Uncle Pete, from the dresser.

"How do you do that?" asked Hunter. "Do you actually read my thoughts?"

"Yep! But only when they're what I would be thinkin' m'self. That feller Nathan, was he what you were expectin'?"

"No, not at all! I thought he had it all together!"

"Well, seventeen isn't very old, though it sounds like it is when you're eleven." This time it was Oma Mika. "And there are so many bad things in the world to trap a seventeen-year-old boy."

"And Nathan didn't have much in the way of guidance," added Nana Rose.

"Aye, you can say that again!" said Uncle Pete.

"He didn't have much in the way of guidance," said Grandpa Green, smiling.

"Grandpa Green, that's lame," Hunter said, though he too smiled just a little. "But, listen, you guys. Were you there this afternoon? Do you know where Nathan lives, and can you do me a favour? Can you go check on Julie? Maybe warn her?"

"I dunno," hedged Uncle Pete, "it's mighty cold out there tonight."

"You're a ghost, for Pete's sake!" argued Hunter. "Ghosts are supposed to be cold!"

"Ahem! What do you know about ghosts, boy? What do you think we keep this here stove around fer? We like bein' warm more than most people!" Uncle Pete was indignant.

"Oh, tell him," Nana Rose said. "Can't you see he's worried? We're here to help him build character, and he's worrying about a girl; I think we should cooperate."

"There aren't any drug dealers on their way to get Nathan tonight," said Grandpa Green. "It was us. I called Nathan's mother and pretended to be after him for a bad debt."

"You?" Hunter was incredulous. "Passing for a drug dealer?"

"Well, I couldn't have done it without borrowing a bit from Helen's college vocabulary. I told you she liked to swear, didn't I? Now I know why—it blows off a lot of tension, under the right circumstances." Grandpa Green had never looked more pleased with himself. "And it was all for a good cause. He'll be so scared, he might just see the light and get out while he still can."

"But you're ghosts! How can you use the phone?"

"We have our ways," said Oma Mika.

Hunter went downstairs to find Helen and Toni by the living room woodstove. He sat down. "I think I want to talk," he said. "Did you ever wonder what my life might have been like if you hadn't come along to adopt us? I did. And I think maybe today I saw an answer. I guess I'm pretty lucky, after all."

It took a little while, but Hunter told them the whole story, even back to when he first began keeping his secret from them about the library computer and Facepage. He told them about his dad, and how disappointing it had been to discover what he was like and how little he cared about his son. He skipped over the part about the ancestors, although without them in the story Helen and Toni must have thought he was a genius to figure all that out! He talked about the strange video game, and how, even though it was exciting and fun, he thought that he didn't want to play it again. He told them that he had been offered marijuana, and that he thought Nathan wanted a customer more than he wanted a friend. But, he said, a friend was what Nathan probably needed.

"Maybe so, kiddo, but that's not gonna be you," said Helen, firmly. "You are NOT to get involved with that boy."

"You don't have to tell me that," said Hunter. "I'm not going to. But, who will?"

Toni sighed deeply. "Some things, Hunter, you just have to let go of and trust to the Universe."

"Is that the same as trusting in God?" asked Hunter.

"That's the way my dad would have put it," said Helen. "He was always saying things like that. There are many things that are too big for a boy your age, or for one person of any age, to fix. When you're older, maybe you'll be a social worker or an addictions counselor, and be able to do part of the work to give kids like Nathan a chance. Or maybe you'll adopt somebody, or just be a great friend. But for now, you aren't going to be able to help Nathan any more than you have already, and trying to do more could put you in big danger yourself. Time to trust in something bigger. Call it the Universe, or call it God, like Grandpa Green would. Just so you have faith in something and can pray."

"Should we pray, then? For Nathan, and for my mum—I mean, Roxanne, my first mum?" Hunter felt very awkward asking this, but it felt right, somehow, too. "I mean, she's really into drugs, I know that now. And she's probably not going to get better. But still …"

"Are you asking us to pray with you?" asked Helen, her eyebrows raised in surprise.

"Well, maybe. I'd ask my dad if I had one like yours," he said directly to Helen. "I think I'd have liked him."

"Oh, he'd have loved you! He'd have been all over you two like, like …"

"Gravy on potatoes? Steeples on churches?" Hunter smiled.

Helen laughed. "Gosh, you sound like him! Yeah. He'd have loved you more than he loved apple pie—and that's a lot!" Hunter saw tears well up in Helen's eyes. "Sometimes I feel like he's so nearby, I can almost hear him now."

"Do you have a picture of him?" asked Hunter. "An old one, like, maybe in his college football uniform?"

"How did you know about that?" asked Helen. "Did I tell you he played college football?"

"Only about a hundred times," said Toni.

"Yes, I do. I'll go find it. Then we can light some candles and say a prayer. One for Nathan, and one for Roxanne, and one for my dad—your Grandpa Green." Helen stood up.

"And one for each of us," said Toni, getting up to get the candles. "You, me, Hunter and Faith. And one for your mum, Helen. And one for my mum, too, and my dad in Germany. And my sister, and Roscoe, and my dog Barkley that died three years ago, and ..."

"You'll burn the house down, Toni! Just a few, please, and one big one to stand in for all the rest, okay?" Helen smiled and squeezed Toni's hand. She reached out and gave a quick sideways hug to Hunter too, who did his best not to flinch or pull away.

Chapter 17: Shadow Boxing

"Faith," asked Hunter, looking up from a lacklustre game of Backgammon, "why do you think we aren't in bigger trouble?"

"What do you mean?" asked Faith. "Should we be?"

"Well, yeah. First, you ran away with Roscoe. Then, I went to Nathans, and, like, almost got into drugs. And the mums haven't hardly said anything."

"That's not true! They said lots! All they did was talk about it, like, for days!" Faith rolled her eyes.

"No," said Hunter. "They didn't hardly yell. Helen hasn't gotten really mad for weeks. Uncle Pete noticed it, and it's true. She's holding her temper; something has changed. Maybe they are just planning, you know, and not saying anything."

"Planning what?"

"To send us away, idiot!"

"Well, maybe we'll get bigger rooms next time," Faith said. "Maybe we'll get the Internet. Maybe we'll get a trampoline!"

"I'm serious! I heard something!"

"When?"

"Last night. After we both were in bed."

"How could you hear something if we were both asleep?" pressed Faith. Roscoe appeared at her elbow, nudging for a pat. She ran his soft ears through her fingers.

"I didn't go to sleep. I had to get a glass of water." Hunter looked at the floor.

"You did not. You were spying again."

"So what?" demanded Hunter. "Somebody has to pay attention and check things out around here. All you want to do is play with that dumb dog."

"Roscoe is not dumb!" Faith drew her best friend close. There was a long, glaring pause.

"Okay, what did you hear?" Faith didn't want to know, but she asked anyway.

"Toni said that we were wearing her out, and Helen said sometimes she wished they hadn't adopted us, after all."

"What?" Faith's eyebrows went up. How could she have missed this? "That can't be right! They weren't even mad! Did they sound mad?"

"No, but they must have been. They said it."

"You're lying. You're just trying to get me upset." Faith felt her anger rising.

"No, I'm not! They are tired of us and they wish they hadn't adopted us!"

"What did Toni say after Helen said that?"

"She said 'mm-hmm'; and that means yes. They don't want us. We are too much trouble for them."

Faith thought for a moment about moving. She would have to change her whole plan for the year and get ready for a new school. It was a good thing, maybe, that she hadn't made any friends yet. Maybe, she thought, it will be a better school. Maybe ... but still, why did her stomach feel so heavy and sick all of a sudden? She took two of Hunter's Backgammon pieces off the board, without joy. Then she bumped the board with her fist, setting pieces flying.

"Hey, you did that on purpose!" protested Hunter.

"So what? It's a dumb game."

"But you can't just wreck it! There are rules—you have to finish what you started," Hunter insisted.

"Why? Toni and Helen don't have to finish what they started. They said adoption was forever, and now they're giving up." Faith wasn't going to cry, she told herself. She pushed the tears back into her eyes with her fingers, then pulled out the mini-trampoline and started bouncing.

Hunter turned away from the remains of the Backgammon game, and looked at a piece of the wall. It was an ordinary wall, but if he looked at it closely, he could find some old nail-holes where pictures must have been once, and a dirty smudge or two that had missed being cleaned. Mostly, he just liked looking at the blankness of it. He waited while the feeling of that blankness entered him, with its calm, timeless, empty spaces and quiet.

Then a cloud moved in front of the sun, and the room darkened. A square of bright light appeared on the wall.

"Look!" said Faith, as the dark shape of a dog's head appeared, barking silently, in the square. Then the dog turned into a flying bird, and the bird turned into a man with a hat, and the man with a hat turned into a penguin talking. Another penguin head appeared to hold a conversation with the first. Hunter looked toward a soft whirring sound in the room, and there was Grandpa Green, running an old–fashioned projector. It looked like a box with a hole through which bright light flooded onto the wall, and two sticks on the side poking up like arms raised in a "V". On each arm there was a flat, round wheel, and one of the wheels had something wound up on it that looked to Faith like black tape, only the tape had funny little holes all along each side of it.

"Super 8!" he declared proudly. "Got this in 1967—the year we went to the World's Fair in Montreal! Want to see Helen in go-go boots and cat glasses?"

"Yeah!" bounced Faith.

"I thought you said you didn't do movies," said Hunter, peevishly.

"I don't do movies of things that happened when I wasn't there," corrected Grandpa Green. "But I just ran across this beauty when I was going through some memories of my own. I loved my home movie set when I was alive! I can't show you your memories, but I can show you mine!"

"Let's see Helen as a little kid!" enthused Faith.

"In a bit," promised Grandpa Green. "We have other business to take care of first."

Nana Rose was still showing Uncle Pete how to make the penguin talk. Oma Mika actually giggled.

"That's dumb," said Hunter. "I don't see what is so funny."

"See if you can do it," invited Oma Mika. "You must know some shadow pictures."

"No." Hunter didn't know any shadow pictures to make with his hands, and he didn't want to be challenged. "I don't feel like it."

Faith watched the ghosts make penguin shadows, and tried to imitate it. "I got it!" she cried, when her penguin came to life. "Tennessee Tuxedo, here!" she made it say.

"Tennessee Tuxedo—that's way before your time, kid!" said Grandpa Green. "My kids watched that!"

"Yeah, well, the Martins had videos of classic cartoons," she said. "And you can see them on the internet. How do you do the dog?"

Uncle Pete showed her, and she practiced until she could do it. "It looks real!" she marveled. "I never even knew about this before!"

Hunter glowered.

"Try putting your hand closer to the light," suggested Oma Mika.

"Whoa!" Faith's dog picture grew enormous as she moved it close to the light, then small again as she brought it further away. "It got big!"

"Yep, but it's the same hand," said Uncle Pete. "Big, small, it's still a shadow. Betcha you could really scare somebody if they didn't know the trick."

"Yeah! Let's find somebody to scare, Hunter!" Faith was into this new game.

"No. It's dumb. It's just shadows." Hunter wasn't about to be budged from his sour mood. Really, he thought, Faith is so easily distracted! The issue was that Helen and Toni were going to send them away and just quit the adoption, after they PROMISED they wouldn't.

"Watch this!" said Uncle Pete, and made the whole top part of a man, with arms. It was complicated, and took both his hands. The man boxed! With some experimenting, Faith positioned herself so that her shadow was the same size as that of the boxer made by Uncle Pete's hands and they faced off.

"Got'cha!" she said. "Right in the nose!"

"Okay, enough violence!" said Grandpa Green. "I found what I was looking for!" There were now two flat, round wheels on the projector arms. One wheel was like a spool of black ribbon; the other one was an empty spool. Grandpa Green fed the end of the ribbon through and out of the projector, so that the light shone through it. He then caught the loose end and threaded it into the middle of the empty spool, which began to wind the ribbon as it pulled it through the projector. "Film! I happened to catch the whole thing!" said Grandpa Green. "I knew this thing would come in handy yet."

"It's a funny thing about living," mused Nana Rose. "There are so many places and events happening at one time, but each person only gets to know about one place—the one that they are in. That's what makes it so hard to understand each other when we're alive; it's like each one is in a different little tunnel moving through life, only seeing one place and experience at a time. Ghosts can travel and move between the tunnels, seeing and hearing much more. But people can't. "

"But technology is a wonderful thing!" exclaimed Grandpa Green. "Uncle Pete got to keep his compass, and fiddled it into a BS-Ometer. Nana Rose still gets to drive her '63 Pontiac Convertible sometimes, Oma Mika has her, uh, what exactly do you have, Oma?"

"My wooden spoon," she said evenly. "And the knowledge of how to use it."

"Uh, yes," Grandpa Green paused. Then he seemed to puff himself up. "And I get to use my Super 8 Movie Camera and Projector!"

"Wait, what about the convertible?" asked Hunter with interest.

"Sorry, kiddo. No seatbelts." Nana Rose was in her favorite pink pant-suit today, with sparkling rhinestones around the neck and down the sides of the flared legs. She pulled down her sunglasses. "Can we get on with this? The bright light hurts my eyes."

"No, it doesn't," accused Hunter, hurt about the car. "You're a ghost. You don't feel pain. You just like the sunglasses."

"Okay, okay, we're ready to start!" announced Grandpa Green, and the pictures started.

Projected on the wall, Helen was curled on one end of the living room couch, with a book in her lap, a pen in her hand and a notepad beside her on the couch arm. She patted the couch beside her and said something, then Toni came to sit beside her.

"You forgot to turn on the sound!" said Faith.

"Oh, yes! Here it is. State of the art!" Grandpa Green flipped a switch.

"Can I move this book?" came Toni's voice.

"Yep. Though just for ten minutes, okay? I still have to make my notes for tomorrow's class lecture. God, am I tired!"

Toni moved the book and snuggled in close. Helen kissed the top of Toni's head, and Toni turned her face up for a quick kiss on the lips.

"Eeww!" exclaimed both children. Faith plugged her ears and closed her eyes. "Tell me when it's over!"

"Okay, you can look now," said Hunter.

Toni did, indeed, look tired, and she was crying. "Honey," she said, "raising these kids is so much harder than I thought it would be. It's wearing me right out."

Helen stroked Toni's hair. "I know. Sometimes I wonder what we were thinking. Sometimes I even wish we hadn't done it. Our life together was so nice, so peaceful."

"See! I wasn't making it up!" said Hunter.

"Shhhhh" said everyone else.

The two women just sat together for several minutes after that, Toni sniffling and Helen looking sad, too.

"I think," said Helen at last, "that this is kinda normal. I've read that lots of adoptive parents feel this way, especially with older kids. It takes time."

"How much time, do you think?" asked Toni. "When will we start to really feel like they are our children? Like a normal family?"

"Come on, Hon, you know that there's no such thing as a normal family. The Cosbys have been off TV for decades." Helen smiled and sighed. "This is our normal."

"But normal isn't supposed to suck," sniffed Toni.

"Who says that?" asked Helen. "We're in this for the long haul; it will take as long as it takes. But there are some really neat moments, already. Like when Hunter lit candles with us; that was pretty cool."

"Do you think it really meant anything to him?" asked Toni. "Do you think it got through to him?"

"What did you want to get through?"

"I don't know. Just, belonging, I guess. Safety, calm."

Hunter, watching, said, "I didn't hear that part. I guess I left when they got quiet."

"Keep watching, then," said Grandpa Green. "There will be a quiz afterward."

Hunter and Faith groaned, but kept watching.

Helen spoke next. "I think that the kids are starting to get it that we love them. I think they feel safe here. But it's hard for them to accept affection, and even harder for them to give it. If it wasn't for Roscoe, I don't think they'd get any physical touch at all."

"Yeah, thank God for Roscoe. They express all kinds of feelings with Roscoe that they can't with us."

"With humans?" said Helen.

"With human parents," said Toni. "I think they find having parents a really strange and hard thing. It must be terrifying for them."

"Well, that's what the books say, anyway." Helen knew a lot about what was in books. "And it makes sense. If we could have had them as babies, then they would have learned to trust us. But their first parents hurt them, and then they got passed around to different foster parents. Every time they loved an adult, they lost that person. I can understand why they would only want to trust each other now."

"Or only themselves," said Toni, thoughtfully. "Or Roscoe. Even if you lose a pet, it probably doesn't feel so personal as if you lose a parent, or a foster family."

"Yep."

"So, are we in over our heads?" asked Toni.

"Yep," answered Helen. "Definitely."

"What do we do?"

"Just hang in there, I guess. Start looking for a counselor to work with us."

"But I am a counselor! I'm supposed to already know what to do!" Toni looked desperate. "Besides, all of the counselors in this community are my colleagues. How can I tell a colleague that I'm over my head with my children? They won't ever recommend me again. I don't think I can be that open with people that I work with, to tell them that sometimes I feel hopeless, or like we've made a mistake that we just have to live through. Besides, there is nobody in this whole town who has specialized training in working with new adoptive families, or with older adopted kids and all of their special needs. I don't think that regular child counseling is going to be right. There is so much that I didn't know before we got into this—how am I going to find somebody who knows more than we do now?"

"But, honey," said Helen, "you are not making sense. We both know that this is normal. All parents get over their heads; not just adoptive parents. People aren't supposed to do this on their own. We have to reach out more."

"I'm too tired to reach out! We don't see our friends anymore; they are all doing the things that we did before the kids came. That's part of what I miss—where did all our friends go? And other parents have no idea. They think we are way over-protective, or over-thinking it, or over-reactive. They see the kids looking like normal kids, and they have no idea what it feels like to sit here open-hearted every day and not get through. Like all this love I have just bounces off them, back at me, and I feel horrible; like I'm a horrible person whose love doesn't fix anything. Or worse, like my love is poison that they don't want. This thing; this rejection—it's invisible. Nobody seems to see it or feel it but us. "

"Geez," said Faith, amazed. "Toni is, like whining."

"Yeah," agreed Hunter. "And I thought Toni was the calm one."

"Shhhh …" said the ancestors. "Listen."

"I think we need to build a new network," said Helen. "There are other adoptive parents around. I got a notice about a camp for adoptive families. Should we register for it?"

"Well, it can't hurt," admitted Toni. "It beats feeling sorry for myself."

"That's the spirit! And if we can't find a family therapist locally who understands older child adoptive families, we'll find one online. At least we can find a counselor who supports you and me to be the best we can be."

"I'm not going to take the kids to a therapist who sees them by themselves," said Toni. "It's family therapy or nothing."

"Why is that?" asked Helen.

"Because, if all goes like it is supposed to in therapy, then each kid develops a trusting and nurturing relationship with a counselor. That's great, but it's not me. It's, like, competition. The kids will talk to a counselor instead of to parents, and that might keep them avoiding closeness with us even longer."

"Or it could work the other way," said Toni. "Maybe if they practice talking over their problems with a therapist, they can do it more easily with us when they get home than if they hadn't had that in-between person."

"Well, maybe," said Helen. "But the counselor really has to understand about older adopted kids and attachment. They need to know how to walk that fine line, of taking the children's concerns very seriously but getting a reality check from us before they jump on a story. I mean, remember what Faith told the police officer? What if she had been removed from us for that?"

"Nobody could have believed that," said Toni. "She had make-up on her face!"

"Hey!" said Faith, insulted. "I thought it was pretty good! I put a lot of work into that!"

"Shhhhhh," said everybody else.

"But she'll get better at it. She won't be eight years old forever," pointed out Helen. "We need a counselor that understands how the kids can have doubts about us, and how we can have doubts in us—and then, not give up on us. We need a counselor who has a lot of faith in us."

"Agreed! We need one who can help to build up our confidence again, and to keep believing in what we are doing here." Toni looked strong for just a moment before collapsing back onto Helen's shoulder. "It's so hard to keep believing," she said softly, as the tears came back and slipped down her cheeks.

"Yeah, I know," soothed Helen. "You wanted to give these kids a happy family, better than what you had."

"Helen, I'd have given anything to have a permanent family like ours; just to feel like I belonged somewhere. I was determined to do that for them. I still am, but how long can they not see what a gift it is?"

"Hey!" exclaimed Faith, "Did Toni grow up in foster care?"

"Shhh …," said everybody.

"Ask her sometime," whispered Oma Mika.

Helen continued the conversation. "I guess I thought that it would be like my family, growing up. I thought about fun things—camping trips and watching Walt Disney and having Christmas and birthdays together. I thought for sure we could do this—between your understanding what it was like to be in foster care, and my understanding what it was like to be happy, we had it covered. But I was so well-behaved. I would never have dreamed of talking to my parents the way that Faith talks to us sometimes. It's so hard to relate to, and to not lose my temper!"

"They're doing the best they can," said Toni. "I talked trash and lied, too, when I was a kid. I know that you didn't, but that comes from having stability. Our kids aren't used to stability."

The film went on for a few more minutes before it ended with a click-click-clicking sound, as the end of the film flapped around with the rotating reel.

"Well," said Faith, "I didn't hear them say they were sending us away."

"That's cos they didn't say it," affirmed Uncle Pete.

"Yeah, I guess you're right," admitted Hunter. "But why do they say we are hard? We're really good, most of the time. I'm really good, anyway." He shot a look at Faith. "I stay out of the way, I don't make noise, I don't bother them or interrupt them when they're working."

"That's right," agreed Nana Rose. "You have always been very good at not being a problem. Even as a tiny one; you were quiet in the corner and didn't make a mess. You've always been very good at what not to do; sometimes I've been amazed at how long you could just sit and do nothing at all."

"And isn't that being good?" asked Faith.

"Well, yes, it is," said Oma Mika. "But they aren't saying that you aren't good enough. They are saying that they feel tired and, oh, there must be a word for it ... lonely. I don't know the word for how it feels when you love your child but they can't show love back. Is there a word for it?" she asked the other ghosts.

The ghosts looked at one another.

"Unrequited love?" asked Grandpa Green.

"Too long a word, and too romantic," said Nana Rose. "We're talking about parents and children, not boyfriends and girlfriends."

"Nope," said Uncle Pete at last. "I can't think of one."

"How strange," said Nana Rose. "I'm sure these people aren't the first to have it. Adoption isn't new, and in old times children often had to move to somebody else's house because their first parents died or couldn't take care of them. They must have had this ... this thing. When the love they feel isn't returned, and the children keep looking away. I'm sure I've seen it before."

Oma Mika agreed. "When mamas have babies, it's like there is a little light in their eyes for the babies, and when they look at each other, the mamas and the babies, the light grows and gets stronger and stronger. The babies, they think that nobody is as nice as Mama—nobody holds them or sings or makes food like Mama. Even when they grow up and move away, they remember their Mama, and their Papa, and they feel the light in them and it feels soft and safe and warm. And the Mama and Papa, they can feel that. It helps them when they are tired, or frightened, or lonely. They feel that the little ones count on them and love them, and they get up and try some more. But if the light goes

out on one side, that is very sad. If the Mama can't love the baby—I
have seen that!—then the light goes out in the baby, too. And if a child
comes to live with a Mama who has it, but the child can't shine back
anymore because its light went out, well, then maybe the Mama's light
will go out, too." She looked frustrated. "How can there be no word
for that? What is wrong with language, when there are so many things
without words?"

"I think I know a word for it," said Grandpa Green. "Hunter and Pete
and I were just talking about it the other day. Way back in the 1950's,
somebody called it Attachment—that's the light babies have for their
parents, and I think it makes parents feel really good when they see it.
It makes them want to take care of their children. But I don't know the
word for when the light goes out."

"Well, let's just call the light Attachment, then," suggested Nana Rose.
"That's the light in the baby. And let's call the light in the parents Care.
And if the baby's light goes out, that is an Attachment emergency. And
if the parents' light goes out, that is a Care emergency. Or something
like that."

"Are our parents having a Care Emergency?" asked Faith, her eyes wide.

"Not if we can help it," said Nana Rose. "That's why we're here.
Remember, we came to help."

"That's right!" said Uncle Pete. "We're here to help this family get
things right for a change."

The ancestors all nodded.

"What do we do?" asked Faith.

"Well, you know what your name means," said Grandpa Green. "It
means believing. Keep working at believing—believing in the good
hearts and kindness of those women, even when they say "no" to
you. Those "no's" and the frustrating times when the mothers don't

understand you; those are just tests. Tests of Faith, you know? You can pass them!"

"And you, Hunter," said Nana Rose. "Hunters for treasure pay attention, study, look and wait. They are patient. They think about what the treasure will look like, so that they can recognize it when they get there. You gotta think about the treasure of a good, strong family. Start looking for clues and signs."

"Hmm ... like a Quest," said Grandpa Green. "Hunter's quest; Faith's Test. We're poets!"

Everybody groaned. Grandpa Green sure liked to play with words.

Still, thought Hunter, maybe this family thing can work.

"Okay," said Faith, turning to Grandpa Green. "You promised you'd show us Helen in go-go boots and cat glasses."

"Right!" said Grandpa Green. "Here we go—1968!"

Chapter 18: Social Worker

Two weeks after Faith went to the police station, the children had a surprise waiting for them after school. It wasn't a good surprise. Toni and Helen were both home, even though Toni had said that she would be at work that day until evening. Helen looked angry, and also like she could burst into tears. Toni looked very serious, with red eyes. Worst of all, there was somebody sitting on the couch, looking at the children with a look of forced cheerfulness and intense interest that could only mean one thing: a social worker had come to call.

"Faith, Hunter, this is Mary," said Toni. "She's from Children's Services. She wants to talk with each of you alone."

Faith felt something in the pit of her stomach that she had felt only once before in her life, when she learned that they were leaving the Martins. Only this time, she thought, it was worse. This time, it was her fault.

"Faith," said Mary, "Can we go to your room to chat?"

At least she doesn't want to take us to McRonalds, thought Faith. "No," she stalled. "I haven't cleaned it.."

"Well, I see. How about you and I go out for a little while then. Say, to McRonalds?" Mary wasn't giving up.

Faith's stomach sank lower and lower. She wondered if it could actually fall out and roll across the floor. She certainly couldn't imagine enjoying fries and a coke. Then again, maybe the salty, sweet food would make this go easier. "Do I have to?" she asked, pointedly addressing Toni and Helen, not Mary.

Helen came over and gave Faith's shoulders a squeeze. "I love you so much, kiddo. I wish I could come with you, but this is just between you and Mary. And yes, you have to."

Oh boy, thought Hunter. Just when you figure out that you want to stay, the social workers come to mess things up. "I thought you said we didn't have social workers any more!" he blurted out, his eyes filling with tears. "We're adopted! We don't belong to Children's Services anymore! We're supposed to stay here!"

Toni approached Hunter, but he pulled away and ran to his room. They heard the door slam and things being thrown around. Helen traded places with Toni, who held on to Faith while Helen followed Hunter upstairs, knocked gently and opened his door.

Hunter had his duffle bag open and was throwing things into it—his football medal, his photo of Grandpa Green, his stuffies, and his favourite books. Tears ran down his face and his breath heaved in sobs. He sat down on his desk chair and cried.

"Hunter, honey!" Helen's voice was gentle, but urgent, "You aren't going anywhere. This is just a check-up. The officer at the police station asked Children's Services to investigate Faith's claims that you weren't being treated well here. It's just routine. They'll see that you are okay, and that will be the end of it."

"Excuse me," Mary was at the door. "I think I should start here, after all. It's important, Ms. Green, that you not be present to influence the boy. I would ask you to go downstairs with, um, Mrs. Green."

For some reason, one part of Hunter found it funny, the way Mary stumbled over the two Ms. Greens, and his next sob came out as a snort. He snorted and hiccupped while the tears, and now snot, ran down his face. He looked around the room for reinforcements, and, there they were. The ancesters were lined up on the top of his bookshelf, under a big banner that read, "It will be okay". Uncle Pete and Oma Mika each held up one end, while Nana Rose and Grandpa Green made hush signals with one finger to their lips. Hunter struggled to control his breaths until they became more even again and he could speak.

Helen gave his shoulder a little squeeze (which he still didn't like), and left the room. Mary closed the door.

"So, how is it living here with these two women?" she asked.

"It's good. They take good care of us."

"Tell me more." Mary waited.

"We're safe. They don't hit us or drink alcohol."

"Are these your clothes?" she asked, gesturing to the piles of clean and dirty laundry around the room.

"Yes. I meant to put them away, but I didn't know anybody was coming."

"Are either of you ever physically punished?"

"No."

"Are you quite sure?" she asked, one eyebrow raising. Hunter was impressed; he always wanted to be able to raise just one eyebrow.

"No. I mean, yes, I'm sure. They don't hit us."

"What about holding? Have either of you been held down against your will? Or thrown?"

"No."

"Good. And, what about affection. Are the women affectionate?"

"Yes, I guess so," said Hunter. "They like us a lot."

"Are they affectionate with each other?"

"Well, they are married to each other," said Hunter.

"Do they kiss?"

"Well, yes. Like I said, they are married to each other." Hunter wondered what she was getting at.

"What else do they do in front of you?" asked Mary, with that eyebrow raising again.

"They dance, they hold hands, they hug. They sit together."

"How do they fight?" asked Mary.

"They bicker a lot. But they make up again."

"How do you feel about their fighting?"

"I don't like it." Then, fearing he'd said too much, Hunter corrected, "but it doesn't bother me that much. They don't hit or throw stuff or anything. They just like to argue sometimes."

"I see." Mary wrote something down.

"And how do they discipline you?"

"Like, when we are bad?" Hunter thought. "They count to three and fine us from our allowance if we don't stop. Or, if it's worse, they talk to us, make us talk about what happened. Or write. Sometimes I have to write about what happened and why I should be sorry. We stay in our rooms until we write about it. "

"Is there anything, anything at all, else that you want to tell me?" asked Mary.

"Don't move us. We are doing good here. Actually," he felt his courage rise, "we weren't supposed to have any more social workers. I know you are doing your job, but you should go investigate some kids with addicted parents they are stuck with. Not us."

That was a long speech for Hunter to make to a social worker, and he felt incredibly brave. He also felt scared. Had he said it right? Should he have said nothing at all, refused to answer her questions? Should he have done what he used to do to social workers, and just looked at the wall or said 'mmm'? Did he sound mouthy, like a bad kid? Talking wasn't safe, he knew that! But he wanted to stand up for Toni and Helen. He couldn't believe that Faith had gotten them into this, and he wanted to pelt her when he got her alone. But he didn't want her to get moved to another family. He wanted them to be together: him, her, Helen—or was it Mum? Toni-Mutti, Roscoe, and the ancestors.

Hunter shifted in his chair, and he must have somehow bumped the bookshelf while he did so, because, to his surprise, a glass of water tumbled over. The puddle flew in an arc toward Mary's notebook.

"Look out!" he said, too late. Mary's notebook and blouse were soaked.

"Oh, I'm sorry!" he said. "I'm not very coordinated. It's because my mother drank alcohol when she was pregnant. I'll get you a towel." He hurried to the towel cupboard and back. As he re-entered the room, he saw what had happened immediately. There was Uncle Pete, smoking his scentless pipe and leaning against the fallen water glass, looking carefree and innocent as the day. Hunter's suppressed laughter once again turned into a snort, so he pretended to sneeze into the elbow of his hoodie.

"I think that's all," said Mary, wiping herself. "Thank you, Hunter, you've been very, very helpful."

"Rmmm" mumbled Hunter, old style.

Now it was Faith's turn. She had been waiting, feeling more and more afraid. Getting into the car with this woman felt all wrong. As they drove off, Faith looked desperately back to the house, to see Helen, Toni, and even her brother Hunter on the front stoop. She longed for a sign from Hunter, a thumbs up or something, but he just stood there, pointing at his shirt. Was this something she was supposed to understand? And where were the ancestors? She hoped they would somehow tell her what to say to make this turn out right.

When they were seated with their cokes and fries, Mary unbuttoned her coat, revealing a very wet shirtfront. She looked down, and buttoned up again.

"What happened to your shirt?" asked Faith.

"Oh, never mind that," answered Mary, irritatingly cheerful. "Accidents happen!"

There it was again, that forced cheerfulness that drove Faith mad. Just to show Mary that they were not the least bit alike, Faith took her coat off. Then, sensing a weakness in Mary's refusal to answer her question, she said, "It looks like it got hit by a flying puddle."

"I'm not here to talk about my blouse," said Mary. "We're here to talk about your home with Toni and Helen."

"You mean my mum and my mutti." A social worker, thought Faith, ought to know better than to talk about a child's parents by their first names.

"Yes. How are things going at the Greens?" Mary held fast to the cheerful voice. This Mary is no pushover, thought Faith.

"It's good. Lots to eat, nice clothes, toys, Roscoe. We even take piano lessons. Couldn't ask for more."

"Then why did you tell Officer Mike that you were unhappy, and needed to be removed?" This Mary person could be direct, now that she got down to business.

"Because. That's all."

"Because why?"

"Because I don't know why. But I won't do it again."

"You aren't allowed to?"

"I don't want to." Faith stuffed several French fries into her mouth to signal that she was done talking.

"You made some very specific allegations," said Mary.

Faith stared and chewed.

"You said that they gave you old, ripped clothing."

Faith chewed, and pointed to her school clothes.

"You said they didn't take care of Roscoe."

Faith swallowed the fries, rinsed her mouth with cola, and said, "I thought you were from Children's Services, not Animal Services."

"You said they were physically affectionate in front of you and that you were uncomfortable with this."

Faith made a face. "I'm eight years old. Grown-ups kiss; kids don't like to watch it. I'm normal. "

"But Toni and Helen are both women."

"It's the twenty-first century, Mary," said Faith, now rolling her eyes. "If you have a problem with lesbian kissing, you should watch TV more." Faith was feeling bolder. Yes, she was being sassy, but hadn't the ancestors taught her that there was a time and a place for extreme methods? And what could be more urgent than this, standing up for her family?

Her family—that's what they were. She saw them in her mind: Mum, Mutti, Hunter, Roscoe, the ancestors. All in a circle. With the Martins and Grandma Green and cousins and aunts and uncles surrounding them in a bigger circle. She imagined these people holding hands, and forming a barrier to hold her in, and to hold danger out.

"Is there anything you need to tell me, or want to tell me?" asked Mary.

"Yes. I really need to stay with my mums and my family."

"So, what has changed for you since you talked to the police officer?"

Faith actually paused and thought.

"Toni—I mean, Mutti, and Mum, say that we'll make it work. So, I'm staying." This is sounding serious, thought Faith.

After a moment's pause, while Mary scribbled in a dry notebook, Faith spoke. "There," she said, "I answered your question. Now, how did you get all wet? Did Hunter do it?"

Mary sighed, then put the cheerful voice back on. "So, are you about finished with that? Want to take the rest with you?"

"Yeah," said Faith. "You need to get back to your office and change."

Back at the house, Faith and Hunter, Mum and Mutti and Roscoe sat close together after supper. "Is Mary coming back?" asked Faith.

"No. Not unless she gets another call from the police, or from one of you," answered Mutti-Toni. "I told you; you're adopted. No more social workers."

"I'm glad."

"Me too," said Hunter. "But you should have seen her face when the water hit—right in the face and down the front!"

"Hunter, that was mean," said Mum-Helen, her brow wrinkled.

"I told you, I didn't do it!" Hunter grinned.

"You should believe him this time," added Faith, her eyes twinkling. Up on the top shelf, Uncle Pete, in full Maritime-style rain gear, was doing a little jig with Nana Rose and Oma Mika, while Grandpa Green played a fiddle only the children could hear.

The BS-ometer, thought Faith, just registered a perfect zero.

Chapter 19: December Meltdown

Faith and Hunter sat in the family room, playing Backgammon and thinking together about the four months since they had come to live with the Greens.

"Just think," said Hunter, "we've been here two whole seasons. It was summer when we moved, and now it's winter."

"Yeah, what if we get used to it?" said Faith.

"Well, that'd be okay, I guess." replied Hunter, with a shrug.

"Wait," said Faith. "We haven't seen how they do Christmas. I'm not deciding anything until I see if we have Christmas."

"Of course they'll do Christmas! What do you think? They're lesbians, not Martians." Hunter defended the new mums more out of a need to put Faith in her place than out of conviction. The fact was, it was the tenth of December, and there wasn't a tree or Christmas light in sight.

It wasn't that the Greens didn't do holidays. Thanksgiving had gone well. The Martins had come over, and Toni had cooked a turkey with cranberry sauce and stuffing and everything. Helen made a mean gravy that more than made up for the fact that she left bits of potato skin in the mashed potatoes. The Martins had brought pumpkin pie and whipped cream. Grandma Green had come. Aunt Harriet, who had been the first outside family member to visit back in August, sent funny cards and a turkey that walked across the table when you wound it up.

Halloween had been even better. Helen and Toni believed in home-made costumes, which had made the children nervous. At the Martins, they had made up costumes out of a big trunk of dress-up clothes that had been gathered, first by the Martins' own children, and then by a string of foster kids. Sometimes their first mother, Roxanne, brought them store-bought costumes that she bought on sale a year ahead. These were added to the trunk. But when they came to the Greens they brought only Hunter's favorite pirate costume and Faith's toy boxing gloves.

Hunter had grown a lot since the year before, and only the hat still fit. "Never mind," said Helen, and she cut a pair of old jeans all jagged to reach just below his knees. They added a big, full shirt and wide belt that she scraped up out of her closet. He would never have worn a large woman's blouse any other time, but it actually worked well. She made him a vest of black fabric, and offered him a skeleton-print scarf to wrap around his head and tie pirate-style instead of the hat. In the end, he tied the scarf to a belt loop, and wore the hat. Then Toni sewed white "bones" to a black sweatsuit as a skeleton costume for Faith. On Halloween night, Toni produced face paints, and Faith gained a skeletal grin. Hunter made a scar on his cheek and pirate tattoos on his forearms. They went trick-or-treat in the neighbourhood, filling pillow cases with candy. The Greens allowed one "all-you-can-eat" night before putting it in the freezer to be gradually distributed. Hunter thought that, all in all, Halloween hadn't lost anything since moving to the Greens.

Back in the family room, with December winds blowing cold rain against the windows and a warm fire in the woodstove, Faith rolled doubles and took two of Hunter's Backgammon pieces prisoner. "Hey, I hate you!" he said, although not as though he meant it.

"No, you don't. You used to, but you don't anymore," Faith replied with confidence.

"How do you know I don't?"

"Because if you didn't have me, you'd be bored. Toni—I mean, Mutti, said so. It's your turn, so roll."

Hunter rolled double four's, and couldn't use them. "Okay, but do you have to beat me every time I teach you how to play something?" he asked.

"Yup. Except football; I can't beat you at football."

"Jeez, you shouldn't be able to beat me in football! You're three and a half years younger than me!"

"Yeah? Well, wait and see." Faith moved two pieces off the board. "I'll bet you three marbles that Mum and Mutti don't have a tree by December 20."

"That late? Sure they will. You're on. Do I get to pick the marbles?"

"Only if you win. If you lose, I pick three of yours."

By December 15, both children were worried. Helen had arranged her teaching schedule to be home after school, but her college students were finishing their term, and she brought home stacks of long papers to mark. Every day when they got home the children found her bent over the kitchen table, writing comments on one paper in between her "to do" and her "done" pile. The "done" pile got bigger, but the "to do" pile didn't get any smaller; it grew by a few inches every time Helen went to the college.

"I'll get a tree when I'm done with my semester grades," she kept saying, but the children couldn't help wondering when that would be. One evening Faith heard, from her listening spot at the top of the stairs, Helen with tears in her voice, telling Toni that "I can't concentrate with the kids here. I've never been so far behind in my marking, ever. This is the worst job I've ever done, and my students will be getting upset. The kids need Christmas to happen, and I just don't have the time to do it!"

Toni reassured Helen. "In Germany, Christmas didn't start until Christmas Eve. It's still early. I don't know whether that is still true about Germany, but it's what we'll tell the kids. Christmas will start on the 24th and go until you have to go back to school in January." Toni, too, seemed to have extra work to do.

Faith couldn't understand why Christmas seemed to make grown-ups so nervous. What isn't to like, she thought, about presents, Christmas trees, Santa Claus, and no school? Christmas is great!

Hunter had other thoughts. "Somebody has to buy the presents, Faith. And putting up the tree isn't hard, but getting the lights to work is. Trust me, it will take our mums hours to get the lights working."

When the sixteenth arrived with no Christmas decorations, Faith decided to take action. She asked Helen for some plain white paper, and began cutting snowflakes. She squared off the paper, folded it in half twice, then down the diagonal to make a triangle. Then she cut designs along the folds before opening it up again. Hunter joined in, and soon they had a pile of snowflakes to tape onto the house windows. Hunter then taught Faith how to make paper springs by pasting two narrow strips together at a right angle on one end, then folding them over and over each other. They made more snowflakes and taped them to the walls of the family room, attached by the paper springs for a three-dimensional look. By the time Helen looked up from her home-work to think about what was for supper, the family room awaited her surprised pleasure.

"Look what you did!" she exclaimed. "It looks like Christmas!"

"Can we watch a Christmas movie? All of us? Tonight?" asked Faith, excited.

"No, honey, not tonight. I've got work to do. Maybe on the weekend?" Helen went to the kitchen to make a stir-fry for supper. Faith and Hunter looked at one another, disappointed.

"Maybe they don't celebrate Christmas?" said Hunter.

"Maybe they're going to surprise us! Maybe they have tickets to Disneyland for Christmas, and they haven't told us!" said Faith.

"Maybe," said Hunter, doubtfully. "But don't get your hopes up. So far, this adoption hasn't exactly been like an "After School Special", if you know what I mean."

"Well, no," Faith ceded, "but that's why it could happen. First, things go all wrong, and then the surprise comes."

On December 17, neither Toni nor Helen showed up at school for the Winter Holiday Concert. Helen had a class to teach at that time, and Toni said there was a staff meeting she couldn't miss at her office. Still, both children watched the audience hopefully. Maybe this was when the surprise would happen? They walked home together after school, dejected.

"Well, they will be there for tonight's performance," said Hunter. Faith said nothing. When they got home, she dropped her coat on the floor and started, her head drooping dangerously, up the stairs.

"Faith, hang your coat up!" said Helen. Faith's door slammed.

"Oh, sh*t, here it comes" muttered Hunter.

The next hour was miserable. Helen told Faith to come down and pick her coat up, and Faith didn't move. Helen tried coming up the stairs and making Faith go down to pick up her coat, but Faith went limp on the floor. Helen counted three on Faith, and fined her quarter after quarter of her allowance. Faith still didn't respond. Helen was getting angrier and angrier, and Hunter held his breath. "You are going nowhere tonight, Missy!" he finally heard Helen shout.

"You don't want me to go anywhere! You just want to ruin Christmas for everybody!" Faith yelled back. "You don't even like Christmas! I hate you!"

At last Toni appeared. "What's going on here?"

"Tag, you are the parent!" Helen hollered. "I've had it with this kid! I've lost my temper and I can't get it back!" She stomped down the hall to her reading corner in the adult bedroom.

Toni came up the stairs to see what was going on. "What's this about tonight?"

"It's our Winter Holiday Concert and Helen won't let me go. My teacher is going to be mad and it's Helen's fault."

"A concert? tonight? What time?"

"Six-thirty."

"Holy Cow, it's five-thirty now and there's no supper anywhere. This family is having a meltdown!" said Toni. "Helen, are you up to going to a concert tonight?"

"It's concert night? Are you kidding? I have a splitting headache," came from the adult bedroom. "I need to take a migraine pill and lie down." They heard Helen start to cry.

"Oh boy, Christmas is so much pressure," said Toni. "Do you really have to be there tonight, kids?"

"Yes!"

"How late will it go?"

"Till about 8:30, probably," said Hunter.

"Eight-thirty! But it's a school night!" said Toni. "What about the little kids?"

"I don't know. They always do it this way," said Hunter.

"The little kids go crazy anyway," said Faith. "You should have heard the rehearsal yesterday! They were screaming all afternoon! And today they kept getting up in the middle of the concert and the teachers had to tell them to sit down and shut up."

"Really? They didn't really say, 'shut up', did they?" Faith nodded, looking serious. Toni went on, "Other than the noisy little kids, how was the concert this afternoon?"

"Okay, I guess," said Faith.

"Yeah," Hunter agreed without enthusiasm.

"Do you like giving concerts?"

"No," said Hunter.

"Yes," said Faith at the same time. "We get cookies and cocoa. But only tonight. This afternoon all we got was candy canes from Jimmy's mum and Rice Krispies squares from the Teacher's Aid. Oh, I said you would bring some cupcakes tonight, remember?"

"Aargh!" Now Toni was losing it! But she recovered quickly. "Okay, Faith, change your shirt and your pants. Wear your red sweater with the snowflake on it. Hunter, put on a clean shirt that tucks in, and your tie."

"Do I have to tuck it in?"

"Yes. And no holes in the knees, either of you! You have, um, three minutes. First one dressed gets to ride in the front seat." She went downstairs to set the timer.

When the timer dinged, both children were in clean clothes. Toni set it again for clean hands and face and hair brushed. "If you want a donut with your soup and sandwich at Timmies, you'll beat the timer!" she called out. Within ten minutes of starting, they were out the door toward a quick supper and the concert. They could pick up cupcakes on the way.

"Are you sure you aren't coming?" Toni asked Helen.

"No, honey, I'm going to lie down and sleep, then hit the papers to mark again. I'm closing in on the end of them."

Chapter 20: Christmas Preparations

On Friday, December 19, Hunter went looking for Christmas lights in the closet under the stairs. He found two boxes, marked "Indoor lights" and "Outdoor lights", and, with Helen's consent, he began stringing outdoor lights on the shrubbery in the front yard. He thought he could do better if he had a ladder, but it didn't look too bad. Faith came out to help because, she said, she had nothing else to do. "I wish we had one of those light-up deer," she said. Toni wanted to take everyone out to look at lights and sing carols at the church, but Helen vetoed it, saying that they'd had one late night already.

On Saturday, Toni took the children to the last Christmas Craft market of the season. It was beautiful, with music and lights, homemade candies and cookies, apple cider, and so many lovely things that people had made. Toni sighed over wreaths made with natural materials, while the children sighed over cupcakes. Toni bought German Christmas bread called Stollen, and the children joked that if the bread was stolen, they should take it back and buy it properly. They came home feeling more like Christmas, but, still, there was no tree in sight.

"We are the only people left who don't have one," moaned Faith, as she chose her three marbles out of Hunter's collection.

"Yeah, and all the good ones are going to be gone," worried Hunter.

That afternoon, as they settled down to watch "Miracle on 39th Street", Faith said, "pause the movie, Hunter, I've got an idea." She rushed off to the sewing room, and came back with large needles, scissors, and a spool of thread.

"I wonder why they have a sewing room," said Faith, "They haven't even gone in there since we moved in! But look, do you remember the time we strung popcorn for the tree at the Martins? Maybe they'll take the hint and get a tree if we do the stringing!"

"Might as well," said Hunter. It took a little bit of experimenting before they got it right, but soon they were stringing nearly as much popcorn as they were eating. "I wish we had something red to go on them, like cranberries," said Hunter.

"Hey! I bet I can find some dried ones!" said Faith, and off she went.

When Helen came in, she gave a whoop of surprise. "I love you guys!" she said. "Okay, let's go shopping."

When the three came home, they had a tree and some wire frames for making wreaths. One of the frames had candle holders on it. "Toni will love these," said Helen.

The next morning, December 21, there was a special church service with children playing the parts of shepherds, wise people, and angels. The preschool children were sheep, one boy made a perfect donkey with long, floppy ears (Faith wondered if he had been Eyore for Halloween). Mary and Joseph were adults, and the baby Jesus was a doll. People said that last year's baby had been real, but that one was a sheep this year, running amok in the aisles and breaking into tears and howls before the wise people made it to the manger. Afterwards they ate soup and sandwiches while little kids chased each other around the Fellowship Hall.

Back home, the Green family grimly faced the empty tree stand. "That tree has got to get up," said Helen.

"Well, you put it up then," agreed Toni, "I've got to do some baking for tonight's caroling at the church."

"Caroling? We were just at church!" cried Helen. "When am I going to add up my students' marks?"

"But Helen, it's Christmas!" whined Faith, who was beginning to look like a child who had eaten only cookies for lunch. "You always have work to do! Don't you care?"

"I don't want to go caroling," muttered Hunter. "I don't sing."

"But you used to sing," said Helen.

"Yeah, when I was, like seven," said Hunter. "My voice is changing. It's embarrassing."

"I can't do this," said Helen as she tried to lift the tree into the stand. It fell onto its side. "The tree is too heavy."

"Hunter, you help her. I'll be in the kitchen." And with that, Toni left the three of them looking at the fallen tree.

"Have you ever done this before?" asked Hunter, doubtfully.

"Um, well, sure. Lots of times." Helen didn't sound very confident. "It's just that, well, the trees were smaller. Usually, we just do the Umbrella Plant, and maybe some pine branches in a vase."

"But this is a tree."

"I know."

"Is it going to fit under the ceiling?" asked Faith, sensibly.

They had to cut six inches from the trunk, but the tree finally did fit under the ceiling. They took turns with the garden pruning saw. Then, the trunk was so short that there were branches sticking out too close to its end, so they had to be clipped off using the pruner. Fitting the tree into the room width-wise was another matter; there wasn't much room left to move around it.

Toni brought in a big plate of crackers, cheese, apples and carrots. "Cookies?" pleaded Faith, batting her eyes appealingly.

"No!" answered Toni, Helen and Hunter together. "This is kid-stabilizing food," explained Toni. "It calms you down, so eat lots." From the kitchen, the smell of chili was wafting, with plenty of hamburger, the way Hunter liked it.

"Okay, here are the lights!" announced Hunter, bringing out the indoor lights box. The next hour and a half were spent untangling the strings, testing and replacing bulbs. Helen put on music, but even so Faith found the going pretty tedious. She sat by the end table, eating cheese and slipping nice bits to Roscoe. By 4:30, it was time to quit and eat supper so that they could go out caroling at six.

"But it's not done yet! And it's scrawny!" whined Faith. Hunter looked at the tree, and, from a few feet away, it did indeed look scrawny. The branches had short needles, not the long thick ones that the Martin's tree always had, and there were large spaces between them where the wires to the lights showed. He sighed.

"Do we have to go out caroling, Helen?" asked Toni. "Maybe we need to stay home tonight."

"But, we always go caroling with the church!" whined Helen. "It's one of the only times you go to church with me! We never miss it! What has happened to us?"

"Uh, we did," muttered Hunter.

"Come to the table, and let's eat," said Toni. "It's a high protein meal; we'll all feel better." No one thought they were hungry, but once the food was in front of them, each of the Greens found that it smelled and tasted very, very good.

"Okay," said Toni. "Tomorrow is December 22, and I have to work all day, and Helen, you still have marking to do, right?"

"Right."

"And, we have no plans for the kids, right?"

"Right."

"How did this happen?"

"I thought I'd be finished by now," said Helen, sadly.

"So, what is Plan "B"?"

"We could go swimming," offered Faith.

"I hate swimming," said Hunter. "How about we just stay home? We'll be good."

"I don't think that will work," said Helen. "Maybe we need a babysitter."

"A babysitter?? We don't know any babysitters!" said Toni.

"Well, isn't it about time we met some?" asked Helen.

The ancestors could look after us, just fine, thought Faith.

"Okay, we'll make some calls. But we aren't going out tonight. It's too much for me, and for you, and for the kids," said Toni. "Lots of things have changed, Helen, and mostly for the better. But we can't do everything that we used to do, and we need to start asking for help more."

Helen looked around. The tree was starting to lean a bit. Around them, the dust of four months without a good house-cleaning was showing; there were cobwebs on the ceiling, and balls of dust and Roscoe's fur hid like small animals in the corners of rooms. Through the doorway to the living room, she could see four loads of laundry piled on the couch for folding, and there was more in the dryer. The children's rooms, she knew, were disaster areas of toys and clothing strewn on the floor. She sighed. "I guess this house isn't anywhere near ready for Christmas. I mean, Jesus was born in a barn, but still …"

"Do you think it was cleaner than this?" asked Faith.

"Maybe," said Hunter.

When she finished eating, Helen got a pad of paper for making lists. Toni went to the kitchen and came back a few minutes later, smiling.

"Okay," said Toni, "Here's a plan for tonight and tomorrow. I called my friend with a seventeen-year-old daughter, and she's available to babysit tomorrow morning, but you kids will have to go to the swimming pool in the afternoon." Hunter started to protest, but decided against it when she glared in his direction. "Tonight, I'm going to dust and vacuum downstairs, and I'm going to sort each person's clothes into a basket for them to fold and put away. Helen, you work on your marking; you have tonight, and tomorrow, will that be long enough?"

"Yes, I'm really, really close. Just a few hours, now."

"Kids," went on Toni, "you can start with your bedrooms. Four piles: Give Away, Put Away, Recycle, and Throw Away. We should have done this last weekend, so we could give toys you've outgrown to Santa's Workshop. But, we can still take them to the thrift store, and somebody will love them. I'll get the bins from the garage, and you can start tonight."

"Tonight?" whined Faith. "But what about caroling?"

"Tonight. Christmas will come when we are ready for it."

Everyone paused and let this sink in. What was she saying? It would come, wouldn't it? Faith finally said, in almost a whisper, "But what if we aren't ready? Will it not come?"

"It will come," said Toni, calmly. "We'll make it. Even if we have to have Christmas in January, we'll have Christmas."

"January!" cried Hunter, "do you really think it's going to take that long?"

"No," said Toni. "I'm just saying, we'll do it in our own time this year."

The next day, December 22, went too quickly. Helen barely finished her grading, but by four o'clock, when she picked the kids up from the swimming pool, she was done. "Woo hoo!" she shouted, doing her happy dance. "Done till after New Years!" Hunter's room was coming along, with Uncle Pete and Grandpa Green swapping stories about cleaning projects and casting their votes about what he should keep and what he should let go.

But Faith was having trouble concentrating on sorting the things on her floor. They seemed to call out to her, "play with me!" even with Oma Mika coaching her forward. Helen came to work with her after the swimming break, and, although Helen tried not to lose her temper, Faith could tell she was overwhelmed by the mess and the lack of progress. "What have you done, Faith? This looks worse than when you started. There is only one thing in the 'give away' box, and your clothes haven't even been folded!" Helen plunked herself on Faith's floor and began putting scraps of paper into the recycle bin.

"I can't do this!" howled Faith, "It's too hard!"

"No, it's not. Here, start with your clothes. Put the dirty ones here," Helen pointed to the hamper, "and the clean ones here," she pointed to the bed. Then we'll fold the clean ones."

Toni came home and served the leftovers from Sunday's supper, and the family decided that they would decorate the tree on Tuesday, after the cleaning was finished. "Okay," said Helen, "but we need to make some progress tonight, because tomorrow I have a project that I want you to help me with."

Tuesday morning, Hunter's room was finished first, so he brought in firewood and offered to walk Roscoe. "No, we'll walk Roscoe all together," said Helen. They took Roscoe to the woods at the end of the street, and as they walked, they collected blown-down evergreen twigs and small branches, pine cones, red berries on stems, and fanciful bits of lichen that littered the ground. At home, Helen added bits of holly to the collection, along with some soft, fuzzy buds of the magnolia tree. She brought out twine, scissors, a hot glue gun, and the wire wreath forms that she had bought on the day of the craft fair. It was hard to get the greens to stay on the wire rings, but Helen helped with this until they had four full wreaths, one with candle holders. Then the children added berries, pine cones, lichens, and buds until each one was an original work of art. They put one on the front door, one on the wall in the family room, and one flat on the table holding four red candles.

"Who is the fourth one for?" asked Faith.

"Who would you like to give it to?" asked Toni in return.

"The Martins," said Faith. "Can we see them this Christmas? I miss them."

"Yeah," said Hunter. "The Martins."

"I thought so!" said Helen. "Let's call and see when they can come. It's a bit of a drive for them, but hopefully they can make the trip, or we will go to their house."

They called the Martins right then, and, since they were closing in on the housecleaning, they felt confident inviting them for the next night, December 23. "We thought you'd never ask!" laughed Ruby. "You folks must be pretty busy over there."

"It's a bit crazy," admitted Helen, "but there is light at the end of the tunnel."

"Yeah, we're almost ready to decorate the tree!" said Faith, and Ruby caught her breath in surprise.

"My goodness! Ours has been up since December 1st! How could you stand to wait this long?"

"Well," Hunter explained in his most mature voice, "In Germany, they don't even put up the tree until Christmas Eve. We've just been doing things more European style over here."

"Oh! I see! Well, we'll come over, but will you come to see our tree after Christmas, and before New Years?" asked George.

"Does it have on my wooden angel?" asked Faith. "And my dog ornament for when I wanted a dog? And the paper chains I made in Grade One? And the Egg Carton Bells?"

"What about my miniature sled?" asked Hunter. "Did you put that on? And the ornament with our picture on it that I made at Cub Scouts?"

"You'll have to see," was all that George and Ruby would say. "We'll be there tomorrow night, and we'll bring your presents for opening early, okay?"

Chapter 21: Everything Changes

The children were excited. "They are going to love this wreath!" said Faith, but Hunter wanted to go shopping. "Can we go tomorrow?" he asked. "And can we each have some time alone with you?" As it turned out, they all went out after supper, when Toni and Helen could take turns with each child. Small gifts were bought by each child for one another, for Helen, Toni, and the Martins.

The morning of the twenty-third went by in a rush of secret wrapping and projects. Toni came home early to cook, and Helen went out for "last minute shopping." Christmas was, indeed, going to happen.

"Shall we have our turkey today, or on Christmas day?" Toni asked. Everyone agreed that they should have the turkey that evening, so that Christmas Eve could go more easily with minimum cooking. Helen straightened the tree one last time, and brought out the decorations. There were boxes and boxes of them! There was even a whole little village to set up on the coffee table, with houses, trees, a skating pond, little people, Santa with his sled and eight reindeer, and a tiny dog that looked to Faith just like Roscoe. In another box was the manger scene, carved of wood and painted by people who lived in Guatemala, Toni said. From Germany there were angels with wooden faces, carved Teddy Bears, and the tiniest band of ladybugs playing musical instruments. There were chimes that rang "ping! ping!" when the candles under them were lit, and that made swirling shadows on the ceiling when they turned. The children and Helen were still putting out decorations when the Martins arrived.

Ruby and George placed several packages under the tree, then Ruby opened a box that contained the ornaments that the children had made over the years at their house. "Here," she said, "we thought that you would want these to live here now."

Faith stared. She felt sudden tears in her eyes, then burning as she tried to hold them back. What am I doing? she thought, as the first tear escaped down her cheek. She turned and ran up the stairs as fast as she could to the privacy and shelter of her room, leaving five startled people in the family room. Only Roscoe ran after her.

In her room, Faith felt hot tears spill down her cheeks. The Martins didn't want their tree ornaments any more. They weren't going back there to live again, ever. Even though she now liked it at the Greens, and even though she had Roscoe, the Ancestors, Mutti and Mum, she suddenly missed the Martins and her old room, where she had lived from almost as far back as she could remember until last August. She thought of the photographs of other foster kids who had lived at the Martins, and she pictured herself and Hunter there, too, on the wall, staying eight and eleven years old forever. Just two more foster kids, that's all.

Roscoe climbed up next to her on the bed, where she lay, face down, her pillow damp with tears and a runny nose. The ancestors gathered silently around, their hands resting weightlessly on her back, so that it was some time before she noticed that they were there at all. She wished that just one of them could hold her solidly; it didn't matter which one. But they could not; only Roscoe was warm beside her.

Oma Mika finally spoke. "You cry, little one," she softly crooned. "There are so many losses in this life. Everything does change. It will be well again, but tonight, you need your sadness. Crying makes room for the new."

Faith's tears seemed to be slowing down, and her sobs had become hiccups. Her nose was entirely plugged now, and her pillow case was soaked through. "Don't they love me anymore?" she finally whispered.

"Of course they do!" exclaimed Nana Rose. "You were their little girl when you came to them, just three years old. Think of how much you grew and changed while they took care of you and loved you. They can't stop loving you now, just as you can't wash all of the things that you did together out of your heart and your memory. They will love you as long as they live."

"How long will that be?" asked Faith.

"No one can say," Nana Rose replied.

"But don't you know? You're already dead, you should know when they are going to die, too. They are old, aren't they?"

"No, ghosts know the past, but not the future," said Nana Rose.

Faith sat up, wiping her nose on her hand. She spoke in whispers, so that the people downstairs wouldn't hear.

"I used to think I wanted to stay with the Martins always. I made a promise that they were my real parents, and that I wouldn't love anybody else that way again. And, I broke my promise. Now they don't want our ornaments anymore, and I think they don't love me, either."

"Is that what you thought? That they don't love you anymore? No wonder you felt so sad!" said Oma Mika. Faith looked up at her Oma, who had lost so many people in her life.

"Always," said Oma Mika, "they will love you. And there are new people to love and old ones to remember."

Grandpa Green had an idea. "I think," he said, "that each one teaches us more about loving, so that if you think you lost one love, well, you can't. Because that one prepares you for the next one, and on and on; each love you have can be deeper just because of the ones that went before it. Until you meet God, and then you will see it all in front of you. Just love and more love."

"Like the sea," added Uncle Pete. "The stream moves on and on, and it can't go back. But the ocean, that's forever."

Faith stared at him. Does that make sense? she wondered. Maybe Uncle Pete isn't very good at deep thoughts. Or maybe he is, and I just don't understand it yet.

There was a soft tap, tap on the door, and Mutti came in.

"Faith? What's wrong, honey? You left the party."

Faith sniffled. Mutti wrapped the blanket around her and then wrapped her arms around the whole bundle, Faith and all. "Ruby thinks you were upset about the ornaments."

"Yeah, sort of." Faith didn't know how she could explain to Mutti what was wrong.

"Did you think they were sort of giving away you, as their little girl, when they gave us the ornaments you made?" asked Mutti. Faith nodded. How would Ruby and George remember Faith and Hunter every year, if they didn't put the egg carton bells and wooden angel on the tree?

Ruby came around the corner into the bedroom, and sat next to Mutti and Faith on the bed. Behind her came George, Mum and Hunter. Jeez! thought Faith, Everybody's here!

"Oh, Faith, how could we ever give you up? You and Hunter don't live with us anymore, but you lived with us for a long time. We love you! We will always love you!" said Ruby.

"But what if you forget us?" asked Faith. "I wanted you to remember us when you put the ornaments on your tree."

Ruby laughed. "But Faith, that's what I thought about you! I mean, I wanted you to remember all our years together, and so I brought the ornaments to help you! I thought, 'Faith and Hunter will remember us now, every time they decorate their tree.' I didn't want you to forget us."

"Whoo boy," said Faith, and rolled her eyes. "So, let me get this straight. You gave us the ornaments so that we would remember you, and I wanted you to have the ornaments so that you would remember us?"

"Yup," said Ruby.

Now Mum, and George were on the bed, too. It was getting crowded. Only Hunter leaned against the wall, watching but starting to smile.

"You better get over here, too," said Mum to Hunter. Faith started to giggle, Roscoe wagged, and the laughter spread through the room.

"Dog pile!" said Hunter, and fell on top of Mutti and Faith.

The rest of the evening felt magical and Christmassy. First, they all finished decorating. The children each chose two of their home-made ornaments from the box for the Martins to take home and keep, and the rest went on the tree. "There," said Faith, "now everybody will remember everybody, for always."

Then, there was turkey dinner. The children set the table with Toni and Helen's best dishes, with a special tablecloth. Every one sat around it, just like at Thanksgiving, and each one named something that they were thankful for. Hunter was thankful that his "old parents" and his "new parents" were all here. Since the parents were taken care of, Faith added that she was thankful for Roscoe. The grownups were thankful for the children, the season, the friendships, and the food. They ate until they were too full for desert, and decided to have pie after opening presents.

The presents were mostly socks and underwear. But Faith's socks had polka dots and Hunter's were in his team colours. The Martins were delighted with their wreath, and with the plate of cookies that Toni and Helen had made that afternoon. The Martins gave Toni some bath salts and Helen some candles, with the suggestion that these could be saved for a special "grown-up time" later.

Helen put soft Christmas music on the stereo, including German carols that the children had never heard before. Pumpkin pie was served with whipped cream in the family room, where they could look at the tree. The coloured lights and the candle flames at last became a blur of soft light, as Faith's eyelids got heavy and she drifted off to sleep. Hunter stayed awake, storing up the memory of this night.

"Faith," said Helen at last, "wake up, honey. You have to go upstairs to bed." As the two children went up the stairs, Faith remembered what the ancestors had said about losing people and remembering.

"We'll remember the Martins, even after they die, won't we?" she said to Hunter.

"Well, yeah. Of course we will."

"Maybe they will be ghosts! Like the ancestors!" said Faith.

"I don't think so," said Hunter. "Unless they are, like, ancestors for our children. Or our grandchildren. I don't think it works with people you really knew like that."

"How do you know?" asked Faith.

"I just think so, that's all."

"Hmm. Maybe so."

"I wonder who will remember us, and if we'll ever be ancestors," said Hunter. That seemed like a good, magical, Christmassy thing to wonder, after all.

Chapter 22: Christmas

On Christmas Eve, the family made cookies to take to friends, made a coffee cake for Christmas morning, and wrapped presents for one another. Helen brought out the stockings that she had sewn for the family way last summer, before the children had come to stay. There were five; one with each member of the family's name on it, including Roscoe. After a supper of turkey sandwiches, they all went to the Candlelight Service at the church. Even Toni went on Christmas Eve, though she usually didn't go to church with Helen and the children. It was a beautiful, "hushy" service, said Hunter. Faith agreed. When they got home, it was ten o'clock, and falling asleep wasn't nearly as hard as they thought it would be before their very first Christmas morning at the Greens.

In the morning, Faith woke up first. She snuck downstairs before even waking Hunter up. The stockings were lined up on the couch, each stuffed to over-flowing. The two mothers had a rule, they said, that each person could open their stocking as soon as they got up, but the rest of the presents had to wait until after breakfast. Still, Faith couldn't stand the excitement of opening hers alone, so she went back upstairs to wake up Hunter.

Together, they turned the stockings upside down and emptied them on the floor. There were big, fat peppermint sticks and chocolate oranges, wooden tops that you twirled with your fingers, yo-yos, fancy pencils, pens with funny tassels on the tops, new toothbrushes, clear bouncing balls with glittery liquid inside, a book of hand-shadow pictures for Hunter and one of string figures (with string) to make on your fingers for Faith. There was a game of Jacks for Faith, and a cloth bag with wooden shapes that balanced on one another for Hunter. There was a small book of mazes to solve for Hunter, and a small book of stained glass pictures to colour for Faith. There was a tiny man with a parachute for each, and little racing cars. There was a two-dollar coin for each at the bottom of the toe, and a tiny teddy bear not more than three inches high.

By the time two sleepy mothers stumbled down the stairs, the children were well into the chocolate oranges and setting the tops against one another in battles. They had raced the cars, flipped the coins, bounced the balls down the stairs, solved two mazes, coloured part of one picture, played Jacks and the balancing game, and flipped a coin to see who got to open the first present. They had also emptied Roscoe's stocking to investigate the treats and new toys (a ball for fetching, a stuffed pant-leg for playing tug-of-war, and a chew-toy that could be filled with peanut butter) before putting them back in place.

"How could you sleep so long?" asked Faith. "It's almost seven!"

Toni and Helen set to work making French toast, coffee, cocoa, and, for a special treat, bacon. It smelled heavenly. Not even presents could make the children want to hurry through their favourite foods.

They were, and this was odd, kind of nervous about the presents. They were caught between the excitement of getting something, and the possible disappointment of not getting everything that they wanted. They had tried not to wish for big things like new bicycles (Toni had said they would get second-hand bikes in the spring, but not now), a trampoline, cell phones, or tickets to Disneyland. "It's Christmas," Hunter had warned Faith, "not the lottery."

When the presents were finally unwrapped, with interruptions of telephone calls from Grandma Green, Aunt Harriet, Uncle Hugh and the cousins, Oma Nachtigal from Germany ("She must be Oma Mika's grandaughter", whispered Faith to Hunter, "With Hannah in-between." Hunter counted the generations on his fingers, and wondered how

Faith figured these things out so fast,) the results were neither spectacular nor totally disappointing. There were many clothes, pajamas, and books, some movies, blankets to wrap up in, and a pretty Chinese Checkers set that the whole family could play. As promised, the mothers had bought no electronics for the children, and Santa hadn't come through either on that one. The old TV set could be brought out, said Helen, for watching movies, but it wouldn't work for regular TV, so "don't even ask," she said.

In fact, thought Hunter, there was something old fashioned about this new family with its wooden games and its ban on regular TV or violent movies. And, although he thought he had wanted video games, he found to his surprise that he felt kind of relieved that he hadn't gotten any. Without video games, he and Faith didn't have anything worth arguing over except which movie to watch first, and that would be over with Helen flipping a coin. He sighed, and wondered how you played Chinese Checkers.

Faith really did want a trampoline, but she also found the quiet to be comforting, as she wrapped herself in her blanket and looked at her books. I don't get whatever I want in this family, she thought. But, I'm starting to get used to that.

Hunter remembered a Christmas, long ago, when they did get exactly what they had asked for. There had been a game console, monitor, and the latest action games for children and adults. He had spent the whole Christmas racing cars on it. It was really fun, he thought. But the smells had been different that year. Instead of bacon and coffee, there had been Faith's dirty diaper and mixed with the fruity smell of cold cereal, which he helped himself to throughout the day. The mixed nuts and potato chips that filled bowls throughout the day had been delicious, and the many toys that filled the charity hampers that year covered the floor of the apartment. Roxanne had made spaghetti at supper time, many people had come and gone, and they had stayed up playing until they fell asleep in front of the TV.

By New Year's, though, the video game set and many of the toys were gone to the pawn shop, so that Roxanne could buy milk and diapers again, she said. It had seemed, for a long time, like the best Christmas Hunter could remember—all those games and toys, and everything that he liked to eat. He had forgotten, until now, the strangers in the house, and the vague sense of danger that had accompanied him even to bed. Those were ordinary, everyday things back then. So ordinary that he didn't even realize until now that they were gone, and he was glad to have lost them.

Well, he thought, this isn't so bad. Just a couple of old-fashioned lesbian mothers. He smiled. He knew that, to many, his two-mother family was new-fangled and strange. But to him and to Faith, it was becoming normal. I guess anything could be somebody's normal, if they get used to it. Maybe nobody is really normal.

After that, the family stayed close together through the holiday time. They played games, went for walks in the woods with the last of the autumn mushrooms turning to slimy mush, and on the beach with the wind howling and making their noses tingle with salt. They watched movies, with popcorn and sandwiches for supper. They slept together some nights, the mums on a pull-out couch and the kids in sleeping bags, Roscoe happily snuggled between them, on the floor. Then Toni or Helen would read not one chapter, but at least two or three in whatever story they were sharing. And every day seemed to have some time in it, maybe just a moment or maybe an hour or two, when Hunter or Faith felt a strange new feeling growing deep in the pit of their stomachs. It wasn't hunger or sickness, though it felt sometimes like it came from that same place.

It's like bubbles, thought Faith, or a really fresh breeze in the summer.

It's a clean feeling, thought Hunter, and kind of like a laugh but not so 'ha-ha.'

Neither of them spoke about it. But they liked it, whatever it was.

Every evening, before reading, Helen and Toni lit the candles on Toni's Advent wreath. There were four of them, said Toni, because the tradition was light one candle each week beginning at the end of November, and ending on Christmas Eve with one candle in the middle, "the Christ Candle." Helen said that her family had done this, too, and that her father, Grandpa Green, had told Bible stories and led the family in Christmas carols most days during the time of Advent—those four weeks when families prepared, as Mary and Joseph had done, for the birth of Jesus.

"So, why didn't we do it right?" asked Faith. "Why didn't we start in November, like your family used to?"

"Well, we were just too busy, I guess," said Helen. "And Toni and I don't really do the church things that my family did growing up, because Toni isn't a Christian. She worships by going out into nature, remember? I guess we kind of compromise. And, well, we just didn't get it started on time."

"So, we do things in our own time," said Toni. "We make new traditions; ones that fit our family. Because we started late, we'll keep everything up until Old Russian Christmas, on January 6."

"Old Russian Christmas?" asked Hunter, wrinkling his brow. "Did you make that up just now?"

"No, I read about it somewhere," answered Toni, truthfully. "But my family lived in Russia a long time ago, so maybe that's what they did."

"Works for me!" said Helen, and the kids agreed. They would light all of the candles, every day until January 6.

Chapter 23: Lighting Candles

Helen named the candles as she lit them, just as she had learned to do from Grandpa Green. "This one is the candle of Faith, for the people who believed in God. This one is Hope, for the people who believed that things could get better, even when they were sad and living in an occupied country. This one is the Love candle, for God who loves the world, and we love each other. This fourth candle is the candle of Peace, because we long for all wars to end." Finally, she would light the one in the middle. "And this one is for the baby Jesus, the one that the people had waited for. It's also for every child, in every country. We are, each one, born to be a special, beloved child." By the end, it felt like a prayer, so Helen said, "Amen," and Toni and the children echoed it.

"Do the candles always have to mean the same thing?" asked Toni one night.

"I don't know," said Helen. "What do you think?" She looked at Toni, and also at the children. But no one answered. Not yet.

It wasn't until the holiday was almost over that the ancestors showed up again. It was early one evening, with the adults in the kitchen, that Faith first noticed the little train going around the village with Uncle Pete astride the engine, laughing. The two grandmothers appeared on the pond, skating, and Grandpa Green was looking up at the little church steeple, which was actually playing music with bells that peeled a soft, "Hark! The Herald Angles Sing!"

"Where have you been?" she asked, as Hunter rushed over to join her on the floor, as close to eye-to-eye as they could get. The ancestors had made themselves very small indeed to fit with the little village set.

"Not far away. Right, here, in fact," said Uncle Pete. "If you could see inside these houses, you'd see a change or two." And, in fact, there were visible changes in the set. A new blue cottage had appeared, even smaller than the rest, with an oil-lamp glow in the window and a red fishing boat propped along its side. Now some bunnies were hopping around, and smoke rose from the chimneys. The deer began to paw at the snowy ground.

"Why couldn't we see you? You aren't going to disappear, are you?" asked Hunter, suddenly worried.

"No, not yet anyway," replied Uncle Pete. "Not while yer still needin' us."

Nana Rose added, "Folks do tend to outgrow us one day."

"How would it be to be seeing and talking to ghosts as an adult?" asked Grandpa Green. "Talking to God is normal, lots of people do that. They call it prayer. But talking to ghosts tends to get adults into trouble these days."

"But do not worry tonight, children," reassured Oma Mika in her old-fashioned accent. "We will be staying close by for as long as you need us. We came to help you learn. One day, you will find your teachers among the living, and then you will know, and it will be you that move on."

Nana Rose looked thoughtful, like she was just figuring it out herself. "So," she said, "I guess that's what happened to my children's imaginary friends! Were they ghosts, do you think?" she asked the others.

"Most likely," replied Uncle Pete, as the others nodded their agreement.

"Well, I always did wonder what happened to their little invisible friends when they stopped playing with them. Do they just go away, or what?" asked Nana Rose.

"I thought all you ghosts knew everything like this already!" protested Faith.

"No, we learn it as we go, just like you learn about your lives," said Grandpa Green. "Some of us haven't been ghosts very long yet. Oma Mika and Pete are the experts; they've been on a few teaching missions already. Rose and I are still learning the ropes."

"You could put it that way," said Uncle Pete, hitching his thumbs proudly into his suspenders.

"Well, that's okay then," said Hunter. "But if you are teachers, what are you teaching us? You don't talk like teachers. Except for Grandpa Green, sometimes—he can get a bit preachy sometimes!"

They all laughed and guffawed, even Grandpa Green. "Told ya he was new at it!" snorted Uncle Pete. "He'll get better."

Faith brought them back to the question. "What are you teaching us?"

The ghosts looked at each other. Oma Mika began, "It's about having your mamas."

"That's right, having parents," said Grandpa Green.

"You've got 'em, we just wanted yer ta know what ta do with 'em!" chimed in Uncle Pete.

"And how to hold on to them," said Nana Rose. "I've waited a long time to see this healing in my family. I want to be sure that you are the ones who will take it forward someday."

"If you choose to," added Oma Mika.

"That's right."

"So, what's so hard about that? They're parents, they give us stuff and take care of us." Faith looked puzzled. "Shouldn't you be teaching them how to do it? Isn't it their job?"

"Well yes, it's a big job, and adults need all the teaching that they can get. But they don't talk to ghosts. They read, ask their friends, and talk to living experts," explained Grandpa Green. "There are books for them. But for you, learning how to be somebody's children, there aren't any experts, or even any books. So, you have us."

"What's to know? We're supposed to love them, and do what they say, right?" asked Hunter.

"Yes, but the love that a child has for their parents isn't just any old love," Grandpa Green raised his eyebrows and took a draw on his pipe. "It's not like loving ice cream, or even loving Roscoe. Most children don't have to think about the Four Pillars of Attachment, because they just absorb them as babies. But without them, well, what's a chair without all four legs? Unstable."

"Four what? Filters of Retrashment?" Faith had never heard these words before.

"Not filters, pillars," corrected Hunter. "Like, columns, or like table legs to hold something up. And not retashment, either. Attachment. We were talking about it before, remember? It means sticking things together, like with glue or stickers or Velcro. Only with people."

"What's Velcro?" asked the other ghosts all together.

"Sticky stuff. Best invention since the motor car," replied Grandpa Green. "Replaced shoe laces. Changed my life." He demonstrated, to the amazement of the others.

"That would have made a whole lot of things easier," said Nana Rose.

"So, what are the four pillars of attachment?" asked Faith.

"Maybe we don't want to know," said Hunter, cautiously. "If we learn it too fast, the ancestors might leave."

"Dont'cha worry 'bout that, son," said Uncle Pete. "There's learnin' to say 'em, and then, there's learnin' to live them. It's the second that takes a lifetime."

"A whole lifetime?" asked Faith, wide-eyed. "Then, we'll always need you!"

"We're here to get you off to a good start," Nana Rose.

"So, what are these pillar things?" repeated Hunter.

"Well, the first one is Safety," began Uncle Pete. "Easy to remember— safety first. Parents keep children safe while they are still growing. Safe from wild animals, accidents, hunger, and, as best they can, illness. Safe from wandering off and getting lost. If you get enough of that from your parents, then when you grow up you feel safe inside, not scared all the time."

"I'm not scared all the time," mumbled Hunter.

"Me, neither," agreed Faith.

"The second one," said Nana Rose, "is comfort. When a baby is hungry, parents feed him. When she has a wet diaper, parents change it. Hurts and bumps are part of life, from babyhood on. If we get enough comfort in our parents' arms when we are small, we get a piece of that comfort that stays inside of us, so that when we are scared or hurting we can always find our way back to it and calm down."

"Hmm," was all the children ventured on this one. But they were listening closely.

Oma Mika spoke next. "The third pillar is encouragement. Listen to the parts—"en", like in here." She pointed to her heart. "And courage. When parents listen and comfort and encourage us, we take that in and get brave on the inside. So that even when we are scared, we have the courage to speak our truth, or to do the things that we need to do in life. We can go to school, grow up, even leave our parents' home with the courage to believe in ourselves."

Hunter and Faith liked that one.

"Just don't put the cart before the horse," cautioned Uncle Pete. "In this Attachment stuff, courage is built from the ground up, like a house. Ya gotta get it all, starting with you-know-what."

"Safety first?" said Hunter.

"Yep."

Grandpa Green was, of course, waiting to tell about his part, the fourth pillar.

"The fourth pillar," he announced, importantly, "is Learning. It's what makes us most human; almost everything that we know, we have to learn from each other. When babies attach to their parents, they watch them closely all the time. They listen. They learn from them, and they learn how to learn! Paying attention, following the lead, practicing and trying again—all of these things come from having parents to teach us our first lessons."

"So let me get this right," said Faith, who liked to get things right. "Four pillars, like four candles on the wreath. Safety, Comfort, Encouragement and Learning. Our Advent Wreath is like that, but it has one more candle in the middle. What's the middle candle for?"

"You're getting it mixed up," said Hunter. "The Advent wreath is about the baby Jesus. This is about humans."

"Jesus was human," argued Faith.

"But you are still mixing things up," said Hunter.

"Wait!" said Grandpa Green. "She could be right!" Everyone looked at him; he was, after all, the Reverend. "It could be both; an Advent wreath to remember Jesus' family, and an Attachment and Belonging Wreath to remember yours."

"Okay, so what is the middle candle for?" persisted Faith.

"In the Advent Wreath, it's the Christ Candle, for when Jesus finally came." Grandpa Green was looking at the wreath, which was lit now with ghost-lights. "In your family, how about we call it the Belonging Candle? Because it's right in the middle of the circle, like where each of you are, surrounded by the people who love you."

After that, when the family lit the Advent Wreath, Faith and Hunter thought of it as a double ceremony, remembering the names that Helen and the church gave the candles, and also the names that the ancestors had given them. On New Years Day, when they were lighting the candles perhaps for the last time all year, Faith decided to try sharing with Helen and Toni the new meanings.

"Safety, Comfort, Encouragement, Learning, Belonging," repeated Toni, looking awestruck. "How did you come up with that? It's just amazing!"

"Well, I guess I heard it somewhere," said Faith.

"Yeah, me too," said Hunter.

"It reminds me of the book I was reading about Attachment," said Helen.

"I think that when we light the middle candle, we do it all together," said Toni. And they did.

Suddenly, everybody got quiet. The tiny lights twinkled. The bunny rabbits hopped. Some snow fell on the scene, and the tiny church bells rang, light as a blessing falling upon the little town. Roscoe's tail thumped on the floor. The children sighed happily.

"I wish everything would stay just like it is now, forever," whispered Faith.

"Me too," said Hunter.

Chapter 24: Epilogue

It is a summer's day in August, and two children sit beneath a big tree in the back yard of their house, playing with their Pirate set. Faith is now nine years old, and Hunter is twelve. He's grown several inches over the summer, and Faith has learned to skateboard. A medium-size brown Border Collie named Roscoe sits beside them, watching the game intently.

Hunter looks up. "I was just thinking," he said. "Have you seen the ancestors lately?"

"No, not since the day I kicked that winning goal for my soccer team in May." Faith likes remembering that day, but she doesn't like admitting that it was the last she'd seen of the ancestors.

"Do you miss them?" asks Hunter.

Faith thinks about it. "Sort of, but not as much as I thought I would. I mean, they sort of feel close by, don't they? Actually, I was just thinking that you're starting to look like Nana Rose a bit, when you're thinking."

"No way! I don't look like an old lady!" Hunter snorts.

"Yes! I mean, no, not like an old lady. Just, I don't know, the way you press your mouth together when you're thinking. And also, you're starting to sound like Grandpa Green, when you start to explain something, and you always start with, 'Well, …'. Just like he does! It's like you're possessed or something!" Faith was laughing.

Hunter smiles a little; maybe there is a little bit of the ancestors inside of him, after all. "What about you?" he teases, "you can do a pretty good Uncle Pete voice, yourself."

"Aye, do ya think so, m'boy?" Faith's eyes sparkle as she tugs at an imaginary pipe. "I'll be goin' out ta sea b'fore ya knows it, won't I then?"

"And what about Oma Mika?" Hunter asks, "Nobody talks like her."

"No, but if she could cuddle, she'd feel just like Toni. And Helen looks like Grandpa Green, only don't say so, cos it might hurt her feelings a little."

"I guess they'll all here, then," says Hunter.

And so, dear reader, we leave them for now. They will have adventures, and each time they come home again to Helen and Toni, they will feel safer and more comforted than before. None of the adventures that they have in the wide world will require more courage than telling the truth to themselves and to their loved ones, but that circle of loved ones will grow until their lives are rich and full. They will learn many things from many people, but no one will teach them anything more important than the lessons learned from their parents and from the ancestors: Love and Belonging will be the foundation on which their whole lives get built.

How do I know? Because if you could fly up above the back yard, just for a minute, and look at it from above, you'd see something. A man in overalls, his rain slicker beside him, a pipe in his mouth, sits on a high branch of that big tree. He's a little bit see-through, and the smoke from his pipe has no smell at all. He is smiling down at the children and the dog, and around at the tree, the grass, the comfortable house. Keep going up, and you will see the whole street, the neighborhood, the town, and then the whole big, beautiful planet.

Uncle Pete knows a thing or two about time, and even a little bit about the future. And he told me, just today, that this story will go well.

Faith and Hunter:
The Parent Chapters

By Serena Patterson, Ph.D. and Monika Grünberg, M. Ed. .

Beginning

The world is full of children who are in need of families, as it is of adults who have a need to love and nurture them. But adoption is a surprisingly complicated way of bringing them together!

Every adoption begins with a tragedy, and many adopted children have had more separations and losses than even a lifetime should contain. Adopting children who are not babies is not a path to be taken lightly, and it requires that the adoptive parents have not only love to share, but also patience and knowledge.

Before adopting, we were professionals with long histories of working with all kinds of children and their families. Monika was a Counsellor who had specialized in working with traumatized children and adults. Serena was a Psychologist who had taught classes in child development for over 20 years. Both of us had undergone a great deal of training to help us understand the experiences of diverse families and children. We were especially interested in early experiences of Attachment; the unique kind of needful love that children develop toward their first caregivers. This special love affects the character of other relationships, far into adulthood and across generations. How, we wondered, was the ability to have healthy Attachment experiences affected by multiple and traumatic breaks during the early caregiving relationships of a child? How did early neglect set the stage for later difficulties in life, and could anything be done to help?

We did our homework; we became experts in Attachment, from the theoretical and research-based literature to the practice of reparative family therapy.

But nothing really prepares a person for the "real thing" of parenthood, and this kind of parenthood is full of surprises. There is surprise wonder and pride at the accomplishments of our children—especially the accomplishments of courage and of love that are not reflected in school ribbons and report cards but rather in the generosity of their hearts. But there is also surprise pain and frustration, as our openhearted gifts of parental wisdom and affection are met with a glazed-over facial expression, a cold shoulder, or an angry curse. This is not parenting for the faint of heart. Nor is it for the ones who look to the faces of their children for affirmation of their parental goodness.

We responded to these challenges by seeking out more training, listening carefully to what experienced adoptive parents could teach us, and turning all of our resources—intellectual, spiritual, family and financial—toward making this family work. Like most parents of late-adoptees, we dropped out of our social life and became one-topic conversationalists. We worked very, very hard, and we cried many tears. We learned more than we could have anticipated. When the joys came, they were very deep indeed. When the pains and disappointments came, our hearts broke. Our bond to one another deepened and our connection to the things that give us strength (my spiritual faith and Monika's connection to nature) grew.

We wrote the story of Hunter and Faith, and these accompanying chapters for parents, as a sort of experiential field guide to the adoptive family experience. Loosely inspired by our own family, the story developed a life of its own. As she wrote the first chapters, Serena read them aloud to us in the evenings. Our children laughed, or listened carefully, or commented on the thoughts and experiences of the children in the book. Sometimes they said, "I would NEVER do that!"; but they usually liked to explain how someone who was like them in some ways might do it. And so, by sharing the chapters and talking about them, we learned more about each other. We hope that our readers will do the same.

The parent chapters gave us a place to say more: to spell out more fully some of the knowledge and advice that we have found helpful, and some of the questions that we, and many adoptive families, still struggle with. There are questions to help start discussion, and a few pointers toward other works and resources.

Chapter 1: The Little People.

This chapter introduces Faith, a willful and smart eight-year-old girl who finds herself, along with her brother Hunter, in an adoption with two mothers, Helen and Antonia (Toni). Helen and Toni are well-meaning and dedicated, but have much to learn about parenting these two children. The children are also well-meaning (most of the time!), and have much to learn about having parents.

In some ways, Faith is an island unto herself. She once allowed herself to accept the love of the Martins, her foster parents. But now she has lost her foster parents, and she can't imagine why anyone would be telling her that she is lucky that this happened! Faith's whole world has changed, and she's not about to let her guard down again.

But Faith is not all alone, any more than any of us are. She makes a bond with Roscoe, a soft little collie with kind, alert eyes. She has her brother, who bugs her but who has always been there and who shares memories with her of a life before the Greens. And she is about to learn that she is watched and loved by ancestors—people from all of her families, old and new, who have lived before.

You might try some of these questions to get the conversation going after this chapter (or make up your own questions, of course!)

Questions:

Why is Faith angry?

Some people say, "congratulations!", or "you lucky kid!" when adoption happens. But Faith isn't happy about it. Why do you think she's not?

What do you find hard about the family that you are in now? What is nice?

For more reading, you may enjoy this book:

MacLeod, Jean, and MaCrae, Sheena (2006). Adoption Parenting: Creating a Toolbox, Building Connections . Warren, N.J.: EMK Press.

This is a very big "go to" book, with over 100 contributors, including professionals as well as adoptive parents, birth parents and adoptees.

Chapter 2: Hunter

Hunter is an 11-year-old boy who is Faith's sister. He has a very different style of handling the uncertainty and moving around of being a foster child.

To Helen and Toni, Faith and Hunter are 100% their children; adoption is adoption. But to Hunter and Faith, it doesn't feel that way. If their first parents and their foster parents could change, then why couldn't their adopted parents?

Maybe because he is a little bit older, Hunter has a different way of thinking about this than Faith does. He doesn't like to think of himself as a child at all; but as someone who has to wait a while longer to be on his own. He doesn't think that he needs anybody to take care of him or to love him. Imagining himself to be grown up makes Hunter feel safe and powerful; admitting that he might sometimes feel frightened or even that he doesn't always know exactly what he is doing would be terrifying, so Hunter does not do that.

Children like Hunter are often thought to be mature for their age; they seem very grown-up and they like to either do their own thing, or take charge. In a group, they may be unnoticed, and adults experience their behaviour as "too good to be real". In fact, underneath the façade, these children often hide significant deficits in skill, knowledge and impulse control. They are inclined to bluff their way through rather than ask for more information, and because they cannot admit to ignorance, their ability to learn from others is curtailed. It is the fear of discovery that keeps their impulses in check, rather than a firm sense of self under the mask. When parents are not watching, they may do sneaky things that come, upon discovery, as a real shock to parents and others.

Adoptive parents reach out to children like Hunter with a deep and publicly-stated commitment, a promise to be the "forever parents". Of course we hope, expect, and long for the time when our children will reach back, mirroring our commitment to this family, this identity, this life with a commitment to be our "forever kids"—loving us back and holding on, as we do, to this family unit. But the older the child is when they are adopted, the harder it is for them to make this shift in their inner sense of who they are. Hunter has been a part of another family that he has held on to in his imagination for as long as he remembers—this, too, complicates his ability to experience himself as being someone else's child. He may, or may not learn to return Toni and Helen's love.

Because she is younger, Faith isn't able to just wish away being a child; but she does feel more independent than most eight-year-olds. She knows that she needs something or someone to protect and care for her. The problem for Faith is that she doesn't believe there is anyone in this house who is up to the job. Rather than hide her vulnerability under a mask of "being good", Faith lets her anger roar, testing the faithfulness of her new parents again and again by "being bad."

Older and traumatized children for adoption come in both of these flavours, and more. Each has his or her own way of managing the fear, and the painful sense of shame (like there is something the matter with them) that lies beneath the surface in a world that demands that they be strong, or at least "tough", at a young age. Their ways of protecting themselves, including their pride, need to be respected, even when they no longer fit the situation. Like an old favourite garment that a child fiercely holds onto because once it gave them comfort, these behaviours will be let go, gradually, when the child is ready. As adoptive parents, we live by the children's schedule, and we live (and wait) in hope.

Weighing in on the side of the parents is this important fact: Both children do indeed long for "real" parents. They long to feel whole and right with the world. Hunter longs for a real, biological father who would love him without criticism and let him take care of himself. He longs to feel connected and perfect, once and for all, but not dependent. Faith longs for parents who would be there always to make her feel good inside, loveable and special.

For now, neither of these children are prepared for parents who correct them, deny them what they want, punish or disapprove of them even a little bit, because they already feel like they are bad and love is fragile.

Questions to get your family talking:

What kind of dreams, wishes or fears did your children have about adoption? About foster care? Or about reuniting with their biological family?

Hunter and Faith have many memories of life before the Greens. What are some special memories your children have of life before their adopted family?

Does adoption feel "real" yet in your family? How long do you think it takes for adopted children to feel like they really belong and will always be part of the family? How long does it take adoptive parents to feel that way? (Hint: For most children who are adopted after babyhood, it takes a very, very long time. Some people say one year for every year old they were before adoption. Others say not until adulthood. A few say never. But most say 'never say never', because even if it happens when you are a very old person, that is worth something!).

Every family has little "Rituals of Connection" that reinforce the loving connection between the members. Bedtime stories, warm greetings after school or work (sometimes with a hug or kiss), playing cards or a board game together, sharing a meal or snack, lighting candles on birthdays, setting a nice table for a festive meal at holiday times—these are common examples of Rituals of Connection, both small (a greeting) and big (a feast). What Rituals of Connection does your family have? How do they make each member of your family feel? (Hint: if there are some members of the family that are new, they may not have the warm, connected happy feelings yet for these times. Don't give up; change comes to the inside of children on their schedule.)

Don't skimp on Rituals of Connection—adoptive families need to reinforce their connection with loving acts every single day. Reflect together and separately on how you show the connection:

- In the morning when you first greet one another

- As you leave for school and work

- When you reunite after a short or long separation

- When you have fought or feelings have been hurt, and it's now time to make up

- When somebody has a special day or accomplishment to celebrate

- When somebody has a very hard thing happen, like the death of a friend or failing an important test

- When someone is hurt or sick

- At bedtime

- When you share your spiritual life and traditions

Chapter 3: The Ancestors

Most of us don't actually see our ancestors, or hear them talking to us, of course. Real ghosts are a bit of writer magic. But many people in the world do believe that the kindly spirits of those who went before us still look upon us with care. Some call them guardian angels.

The ancestors in this story offer the children three powerful things that they can't believe in yet when it comes to trusting Helen and Toni, their parents.

First, the ancestors do not judge the children; they just accept. When we understand another person, deeply and truly, we usually find it easy to feel empathy and compassion. These ancestors, wise and seeing, are truthful but always with compassion and empathy. It is easier for our young heroes to believe in ghosts than it is for them to believe in the non-judgemental acceptance of new parents.

Secondly, the ancestors connect the children's many "family trees" together, and show them that they don't have to choose between one heritage and another in sorting out who they are. The ghosts help to soften the loyalty conflicts, especially for Hunter, who remembers his first family very well and may worry about betraying them if he loves another set of parents.

Third, ancestors are eternal. Faith and Hunter know too well, too early, that nothing in life can really be counted upon to last—unless we can have faith in something beyond what we see, hear and touch right now. Adopted and especially traumatized children often take a special comfort in rituals of religious faith, and/or in believing in guardian spirits who look upon them in love.

The ancestors have much to teach Faith and Hunter with their words, but they also teach just by being there: none of us are truly alone or unloved. There is comfort and kind company in the universe.

Family Questions:

Who are some of the ancestors of your own family? Are there some you would like to know? Who would each member of the family choose, if they could, to be a ghostly friend? Why?

Are all ancestors related to us biologically? Or are there other people who we might think of as our ancestors, and why?

Some people choose role models from history to be like ancestors to them: that is, to inspire them in their own lives. Does anybody in your family have a favourite hero from history, or even from their past, who they like to think of as a role model, or a spiritual ancestor? (Hint: this may be somebody who is very different from us, on the surface, but with whom we feel a special affinity. One of Serena's mentors from history is Dr. Martin Luther King, Jr., a famous African American preacher who inspired and led the American Civil Rights movement in the 1960's. Another is the writer Mark Twain. Monika, who co-wrote these chapters, feels a special connection to the great French feminist Simone de Beauvoir, and to the composer Chopin, because his music makes her cry!)

Chapter 4: A Breaking Storm

Faith's anger causes something truly awful to happen; Helen gets hurt and Faith knows she is in really big trouble. She looks for a place to be alone again, out of sight. But she's not really alone—remember, there is love out there, surrounding us even when we can't see it. Uncle Pete shows up so that she can know this is true.

With Uncle Pete's help, the readers get to learn a little bit of Faith and Hunter's story. Together, they remember what it is to be cold, and scared. It's hard for Faith to swallow her pride and come back into the warm house. Uncle Pete helps her to sneak in without being seen right away.

It can be very hard to find the right time to tell the stories of our children, and for them to tell their own stories. Every adoption starts with a sad story; a tragedy about someone who could not, or who decided they would not, keep and raise their child. Children need so many things besides love—shelter and food and safety and attention and learning and comfort. Not everyone is able to provide all of these things for as long as it takes for their child to grow up. When they can't, it is very sad.

When adoption happens, some children and parents may not want to think about the sad parts anymore. Others want to think about them all the time. And still others think about them when they don't want to, or can't remember them even when they do want to. Each person's birth and early family story belongs to them, and deserves to be remembered and told with kindness and respect.

Faith's story comes out in small bits. Then, she changes the subject when she's had enough. Uncle Pete is kind and patient in letting her change focus; stories often come a little bit at a time.

Reading this story together is one way of inviting your children's stories and memories, and also what you know about their origins, into the family that they have now.

Some family questions:

How will Faith and Helen make up? Will they? What makes you think so (or not)?

What is it like for your child when they do something that they know is bad? Are they afraid, embarrassed, angry? Do they want to disappear from view, like Faith?

Maybe this is a good time for parents to tell a story about when they got into trouble, and how they got "back into the house" with their own parents.

When we're in trouble, do we feel "out in the cold"? Sometimes being in the family is like being warm all over. But if we let ourselves feel that wonderful warmth, the cold might feel colder still. What does it take to get the warmth back?

Chapter 5: Coming Down a Peg

In this chapter, Faith ponders what her punishment will be. The ancestors have their ideas, beginning with the "old fashioned" idea of spanking.

Spanking is a fascinating topic among children, and especially among children who have been physically abused and/or spent time in foster care. The rules for foster parents are clear and absolute: no striking the children. A foster parent who makes a habit of spanking, or of handling children roughly, is likely to lose their job in shame. Most foster children are aware of this, and they hold fast to this knowledge that hitting children is off-limits.

Beyond trusting in it for their safety, seasoned foster children may learn to use the 'no spanking' rule as a source of power. Getting an authority figure to lose their temper can reset the balance of power in favour of a child who knows they are physically untouchable, and it can instantly change the topic of conversation from the child's shortcoming to the failure of the parent to remain placid.

It may be difficult to believe that children could be calculating and manipulative this way, but considering it from the child's point of view it is just good common sense. Knowing and practicing whatever powers we have been given is a healthy part of growing up. Why is it "good" when a child experiments with their power to use building tools and paints, but "bad" when the same child experiments with their power to predict and control our emotions and actions? It's the same impulse, and it takes many years to learn and to apply good ethics in how we influence others. For mistreated children, these ethics will need to be cultivated through many years of kind, fair and sensitive reactions to what they do, and through many, many conversations about the rights and wrongs of treating others.

Why not stay and try to reason or reassure a child who is mid-melt-down? Because a mid-meltdown child can't hear reason or reassurance. Neurologically-speaking, they are working from the midbrain; the source of raw emotion.[1] The frontal lobes and the language-processing parts of the brain are shut down during a tantrum; there is just no reaching them. If the child is small and can be safely held, this might work (it works for babies and toddlers). But if the child fights off physical comfort, all the parent can do is to make the situation as physically safe as possible and wait.

It can be difficult to hold our tempers as parents when adopted children "push our buttons" for anger. But the stakes are very high; we can't afford to strike them or even to yell. "They can dish it out, but they can't take it," I have often thought; and this is true. The best strategy is often to walk away from a child when their behaviour is out-of-control and we feel our tempers rising. Better to let things cool down than to risk having a midbrain-to-midbrain, meltdown-to-meltdown parent-child situation.

Later, when the child is calm, we can help them to reflect upon what happened. Psychologist Daniel Hughes[2] has an acronym for the attitude that works when reaching out to a child who has had a meltdown: PACE. It stands for Playful (as in light-hearted), Accepting (no shame, no blame), Curious, and Empathic. Truly curious questions in an emotionally safe atmosphere can help the child to re-tell what made them so upset in the first place. Repairs may still be needed; fixing what we break is good ethics and teaches the child that they are capable of mending relationships. Reparations raise us up; punishment or shame tear us down.

Faith notices her emotions, but doesn't quite know what to make of them. Children with histories of neglect or mistreatment usually have great difficulty recognizing and naming their emotions, with the exception of anger—which is rage, actually.(Rage is an anger that doesn't have a clear focus or call for fairness. Rage is less connected than anger is to the thinking part of the brain, and it is therefore apt to lead to more destructive and misdirected acts than is anger.)

Is Faith afraid? Does she feel ashamed? Guilty? All of these emotions are closely related, but guilt is the most complex and late-developing one of the list.[3] Rage and fear are more common among young children, whose abilities to calm themselves, access the thinking parts of the brain, and imagine being in the place of their victims are all under construction. Children who have experienced neglect, abuse, abandonment and other relationship-based traumas have much heightened experiences of shame and fear, often covered by unfocussed, irrational anger and bravado.[4]

For the mistreated and neglected child, learning to feel and respond to simple guilt is a very long-term and high goal. Fear and shame will be what Faith is most aware of; therefore, she will want very much to hide and/or 'get even' long before it occurs to her to be sorry and to make amends.

It can be hard for adoptive parents to deal with a child who does not know what guilt feels like or how to respond to it responsively. Adoptive parents tend to be especially conscientious people themselves, and they might panic and wonder whether their children will ever have a guiding moral conscience. It is important to remember that even among the most kind and moral people we can think of, the seeds of this morality were once not only empathy, but also shame and fear. It is a learning process to shape these self-centered emotions into other-concerned morality. As adoptive parents, that's a big part of the job we signed on for.

Some questions to start the family talking after this chapter might be:

Who in your family remembers being in big trouble with parents? Were they spanked? What other punishments have you experienced? (Grown-ups should probably take the lead on this conversation, perhaps describing some of the ways their parents used punishment when they were growing up.) How did they feel?

Can each parent tell a short story about a "good" punishment that they learned from once? Can anyone else?

Do families have to use punishment?

What is the difference between a punishment and a consequence?

How does your family deal with behaviours that aren't allowed, like hitting and name calling, or doing unsafe things?

What would you do if you were Helen? What would you do if you were Faith?

What does Helen do in the story? How does this turn out?

Do you think that Faith learned something from Helen's response? Why or why not?

Chapter 6: It's A Good Thing

Did you ever notice how many books that are written for children Faith and Hunter's ages have no parents in them? It's exciting for most children to imagine themselves figuring out solutions to their problems and challenges, so many authors start their stories out by "getting rid of the parents" somehow—having children be shipwrecked, or run away, or left behind, or sent to boarding school. Anything to keep parents out of the way of the story, so that the children can experience themselves as stronger and more clever than anyone could have imagined they were. Ever see a Disney princess with a mum?

This story starts in just the opposite way. Instead of figuring out how to get by without adults helping and telling them what to do, Faith and Hunter have to figure out how to get along with parents to help them and tell them what to do. Which do you think is harder? Which would be harder if you had once had parents, but you had to be removed by social workers? That's right—reaching out is terrifying.

This sometimes takes adoptive parents by surprise, because they may have seen the same child before adoption being very solicitous of attention, care and help from near-strangers. Charming help out of strangers is a survival strategy. Help from strangers comes to these children with "no strings attached"; no requirement that they love or trust in return. The child feels in charge of the relationship with a stranger or acquaintance.

It takes a big scare to get Faith to reach out to Helen and Antonia. Such a child will reach out only when it is scarier to be alone than to ask for help. These moments are gold for the adoptive family, where bonds of Attachment[5] are being made very slowly. When the child has a need, or a pain, and the new parents can answer that need or pain with comfort and relief, then the bond gets a little bit stronger.

At first, reaching out to parents for help is very, very hard. One of our children didn't tell us for a very long time when she was feeling sick; it was only by hearing her throw up (every so quietly!) in the toilet that we knew she needed us. If it hadn't been for that one "plop!" picked up by experienced parental ears, we would have missed one of our first and best times to say, "We're here now. You aren't alone. We can make it better."

Until adopted children have had many experiences of their new parents actually helping them out of distress, they have no inner reason to treasure these parents or to follow their leadership. If they obey, it is because it is in their own best interest, not because they trust, love or respect the parent. That comes gradually.

By calling out and being comforted and fed by Helen, Faith has taken a big step toward attaching to her new parents. Will this be all it takes? Of course not! Faith is obviously no push-over!

Questions to get you talking:

How new is your family? Have your children reached out for comfort or help yet? Tell some stories about each person in your family reaching out. Be sure to notice how much courage it takes to let someone else know when we're having trouble and need help—and to congratulate the ones with that kind of courage!

What do you like most, giving help, or asking for help?

What happens if somebody asks you for help and you can't solve the problem by yourself?

Chapter 7: Hunter's Secret

There are three big issues in this chapter:

- The child's relationship with his biological family after adoption

- Hunter having a big secret from his adoptive mothers, and

- A child's wish to have a father

The father issue will be picked up in notes for Chapter 8. The relationship with biological family and previous foster families will be picked up in notes for Chapter 21. Here, we will take on secret-keeping.

Keeping secrets. Keeping a secret from Helen and Antonia does not seem unnatural to Hunter. Hunter has had secrets from adults all of his life; his survival and well-being may have even depended upon keeping such secrets. Nonetheless, secrecy and lying are two things that drive foster and adoptive parents crazy!

It is tempting to give adopted and foster children opportunities to build trust through independence, or to show them early on that "we trust you" by exposing them to temptations before we really know that they can handle it. When they let us down, it's important to remember that they haven't developed strong, internal reasons not to let us down; and that's not their fault. Children will naturally wish to keep a failure of impulse control a secret, rather than face possible punishment, embarrassment, and the disappointment of their adoptive parents.

Until Attachment bonds have had a chance to slowly grow, it helps to keep things very, very transparent and calm around the adoptive home and family. Oversight by adoptive parents doesn't have to be intrusive, but we do need to loiter close by just about all the time for safety's sake.

There is another reason, besides staying out of trouble, why late-adopted and foster children sometimes keep secrets from their parents. Sometimes, having a secret can be a way of saying to oneself, "I belong to me alone; you do not own me!"

It is like each of us has a private room inside of us that is entered by invitation only. Children whose safety has been violated through abuse are especially protective of that private space. For this reason, it is important to show respect for the secrets of children, even as we worry and look after their safety.

It's a fine line for parents to walk, asking "Do I, or do I not read this diary? Do I, or do I not look under my child's bed? Do I, or do I not insist he tell me what this drawing means?"

A third reason why adoptive children sometimes keep secrets from adoptive parents is because someone—often a member of their previous family, has told them to do so. Anyone asking your child to keep a secret from his or her adoptive parents is engaging in behaviour that is designed to undermine the adoptive relationship. Learning that your child has been engaging in contact while being expressly forbidden to tell you so is a red flag for adoption interference or for the child being recruited into activity that will be harmful to them emotionally if not physically. This is a behaviour that should be taken very seriously.

Important! If you discover such a relationship in your child's life, get professional help immediately.

One thing that can help is to steer children toward safe and healthy experiences of secret-keeping. We all keep secrets about gifts and surprises that we prepare for others, for instance. Diaries can be great places of privacy (or, for children who don't write, a box of special treasures they collect) but need certain rules for clarity. In our house, diaries need to be kept completely out of sight; if they are left out "accidentally on purpose", we read them just in case there is something there that the child needs for us to see. Rooms and under the bed tend to be private but are also open to safety and hygiene inspections at any time. Mostly, we rely upon our intuition in steering between neglecting what might be important to know, and prying about what might be important for the child to incubate in private for a while. A good line is, "I hope you will tell (show) me when you're ready; I'd really like to hear (see) it!"

Family questions:

- Start with parents and tell stories about secrets you've had. Why did you keep the secret? What happened when you told? (You might want to keep these stories light and funny at this point; there is enough heaviness in Hunter's story for one evening).

- If you had an imaginary secret box inside of you, what would it look like?

- Would you like a secret place where only you could go? What would the best secret hideout in the world look like?

Chapter 8: After the Game

Hunter wants a father. Of course he does. Who wouldn't want one? In most cultures, fathers are supposed to be there, to protect, provide for, and teach youngsters about life. They also give children a sense of belonging in the world. In Canada and the United States, it is usually the father who gives a child his or her last name. That's important. Hunter is sad that he doesn't have this in his life. Not being openly claimed by a father is a big disappointment to a child, and not even ancestors have the right words to make those feelings go away.

This chapter also talks about how children come about; what we used to call "the facts of life." "When two people love each other very much, the woman gets to have a baby" works fine in families where the mother and father live happily every after together; but adopted children intuitively know that it can be more complicated than that. Adoptive parents need to be prepared to talk about sex fairly explicitly, and with a tactful, matter-of-fact tone. A little bit of humour always helps. Meg Hickling, a Canadian sex educator, has written wonderful books for both children and parents to help us with this.[6]

Birth parents, and especially birth fathers, can acquire almost mythical status in the imaginations of children. What is it that makes someone "your father" they wonder. Is it magic? Is it God?

In his attempts to take the sting out of Hunter's pain, Grandpa Green shares his own Christian faith. In writing this, Serena feared that some families might be put-off by the blatant Christianity. It's not the faith of choice for everyone! But she went ahead with it for two reasons.

First, she modeled Grandpa Green upon her own father who was a Presbyterian pastor and whom she still can "hear" speaking clearly as she writes. It felt wonderful to her to re-create this man's kind voice in this character. Second, most families do find some form of spiritual faith to be important. It is just these moments when a source of pain cannot be mended in any simple way that we turn to our deeper resources of faith. We hope that families reading the book will use Grandpa Green's words as a springboard to talk about and to explore their own faith, spirituality, or meaningful beliefs.

This chapter sets out to de-mystify things a little. We also hope that talking about father-loss will help to take some of the private sting away from it. Alas, some things just hurt, and all we can do is try to be there as an accepting and loving witness.

Family questions:

- Do you have a father? More than one?

- What do fathers do? Why do children who don't have fathers want one?

- Does everybody want a father? Why might somebody not want one?

- What would the best father in the world be like?

- What would the best mother in the world be like?

- What about medium-good fathers; what are they like? And medium-good mothers?

- Hunter and Faith have two mothers in their new family, but they had a mother and a father in their foster family. Some children have just a mother, or just a father. Some have two fathers. Some live part of the time with one parent, and part of the time with another. What do families that you know look like? Does it matter? Why or why not?

Chapter 9: That Darn Baby

Babyhood is a very important time of life. It is when we learn what to expect of relationships—will we be taken care of? Punished? Ignored? Kept safe? What happens when we cry for help? Ask for a drink? Poop our pants? Are we important in the world? Do our needs and feelings matter?

The lessons learned in babyhood aren't remembered in the same way as later life events. They are encoded in our brains and bodies as patterns of sensory impressions, body movements, emotional states and expectation; without a necessary story to tie these together.

Here is an amazing example of such a sensory-movement-emotion-expectation memory in action. A group of researchers at the University of California at Los Angeles in the 1970's were studying the memory of infants. They began by bringing six-month old babies to their lab and teaching them a "game" of catching a rattling Big Bird finger puppet in the light, and then in the dark. Two years later, the children returned. None of them "remembered" having been there before, and none of them guessed correctly which of several toys (including the puppet) they were going to play with. In terms of ordinary memory, these children were no different from another group of two-and-a-half year olds who had never been to the lab before—until the game began. When the lights went out and the toy was rattled nearby, the children who had been there before immediately caught on to the game of reaching out and grabbing "that noisy Big Bird"; none of the children who had not been there before knew what to do. But that isn't all—half of the "new" children had to be taken out of the dark room immediately because they feel apart emotionally. This was, after all, a strange room with a strange person and somebody had turned the lights out! Only two of 18 of the experienced babies had to leave the room; the rest jumped right in to the task at hand, presumably with gusto. They didn't "know" that they had done this before, but they had a body memory that said, "this is safe and you know what to do!"

We call these sensory-motor memories with emotional conditioning "implicit memories." If one short experience with a bunch of research-ers could produce such a strong impression that it would appear two years later with no practice in between, just imagine what kinds of implicit memories are laid down at home, day after day, with mamas and papas and siblings and pets! Implicit memories go on to shape our expectations, actions, likes and dislikes. Unless some very powerful experience comes along to challenge and change one's first, implicit lessons about life, they remain as guides that become self-fulfilling prophecies.

Well-cared-for babies like Max form implicit memories that they matter, that mamas and papas are good, and that other folks are friendly. If they have a good time with Grandpa at six months of age, they will probably be very happy to see him again when they are two, even if they don't "remember" the first visit. Grandpa will somehow just feel, look and smell right to them, and the two will pick up the relationship where they left off.

Meanwhile, every time Max needs comfort or food and his mama or papa comes through, his Attachment love for them grows. It also grows when he looks to them for a "what's going on here?" message, and they look back to signal him that "all is well," or "stay right there—I'm coming!" Attachment is actually built upon our ability to form these implicit memories, and to string them together as the unique blend of sensory and motor experiences that feel, smell, look and sound like "love."

Neglected and abused babies form implicit memories of a different kind. Hunter's experience of babyhood taught him that "nobody helps when you feel pain, so you might as well stop trying to get their attention," and "people who take care of you also hurt you," and "I am basically alone in this world." No wonder Hunter feels awkward and resentful around babies!

I love how Faith, the ancestors and the adults all come together to help when Hunter has his memory. With a little bit of writer-magic, I could give Hunter what all traumatized people wish for—a video recording of the event to clear up the confusion about what really happened, a way of talking about it, and loving hands and voices to help to repair what went wrong so long ago. Now that Hunter's implicit memories are explicit (that is, out-loud and 'real'), he can begin to change the expectations and behaviour patterns that have grown from them.

In the real world of adoption, the stories that could help us to make sense of our children's behaviours and expectations are often not available to us. Sometimes the absence of a story is the child's most powerful story; having to live with not knowing. Other times, there is a story to tell, but it is such a hard one that the adults fear to tell it.

Children need their life stories, right down to when they were babies (and even before that). Most children will ask for their stories, beginning with "tell me about the time when I ...", and they love to hear the same ones again and again. Photo albums and baby books are treasured in most houses. This is not only because the memories are happy ones (often they are not), but because they are real.

Questions:

What does your family know about the babyhood of each member?

If you missed your child's babyhood, tell about what you would have liked to have done or been there for. Don't focus only on the painful;

pick some light-hearted things too. What cute things do you think your child must have done that would have made you laugh?

Chapter 10: Messing with Brains

The more we learn about fetal exposure to alcohol and drugs, the more convinced we become that history itself has been shaped by these things.

The effects of alcohol on the brain may be obvious or subtle, big or small. The range of possible effects is like a smorgasbord of bad possibilities; which aspects of brain and body growth are affected depend upon how much was consumed, when in the pregnancy, how healthy the mother was, and what kind of genes and personal history she herself had. Even the father's drinking alcohol or using drugs can affect how the child develops before, and after it is born. It isn't only that alcohol and drugs cross the mother's placenta and are consumed by the tiny fetus; alcohol (consumed by the mother or, before conception, the father) interacts with the child's genetic code even before it begins to develop. [7]

Possible consequences of FASD may include one or more of the following:[8]

- Poor control of attention in the form of distractibility and/or inability to shift (perseveration).

- Hyper-reactivity or hypo-reactivity to certain kinds of sensations (sounds, touch, smell, taste, light, and/or body movement).

- Difficulty putting experiences into words (a verbal learning disability).

- Difficulty with non-verbal problem solving (a non-verbal learning disability).

- Trouble modulating one's emotional arousal (big mood swings).

- Difficulty reading other people's emotions accurately, or anticipating how others will react to something that the child says or does.

- Having a "one-track mind" that finds it impossible to multi-task, or to hold more than one instruction in mind.

- Being so "in the moment" that one fails to link present actions with consequences for the future or with things that happened in the past.

- Difficulty planning and following through with complex actions (like homework, or cleaning one's room).Being very suggestible (socially gullible).

- Sleep disorders.

- Hyperactivity.

- Poor impulse control (acting or speaking before one thinks).

Secondary effects (those caused by the social consequences of neurological weaknesses) may include Depression and Anxiety, Oppositionalism (beginning as a "full stop" response to feeling overwhelmed), behaviour problems (because it's sometimes better to appear badly behaved than to feel stupid), and an even greater difficulty attaching to adoptive parents.

And yet, there are many things that FASD is not. The preventability of FASD should never imply that the child should have been prevented. Everyone has a right to know that they belong in the world. FASD is challenging, but people with FASD can have wonderful talents, tender and responsive hearts, and strong, loyal bonds with their loved ones.

Here are eight common myths about Fetal Alcohol Spectrum Disorder that every adoptive parent—make that every person—should know how to dispute.

1. You can tell a person with FASD by the way they look. During certain key times in fetal development, exposure to alcohol alters the development of facial features slightly, leading to the characteristic flat upper lip, small eye sockets, short nose, small head circumference and/or other "typical" FASD features. A pediatrician may even use the presence of these characteristics to diagnose suspected FASD, using a special set of measurements and guidelines. However, not everyone whose development is affected by alcohol exposure shows the characteristic facial features;. The timing for developing these features is very specific, and if the mother did not use alcohol during that time, the facial features will not be affected. Also, some families have genetic features that make the FASD influence difficult to detect, even with the tools that pediatricians have. If a pediatrician analyses a child's face and does not positively identify FASD features, there is still a chance that the child's brain and/or joints are affected.

2. People with FASD have low intelligence.. The idea that FASD was characterized mostly by sub-normal intelligence is out-dated. Many people with FASD are very intelligent, although their intellectual abilities are often uneven. Some are very well spoken, giving the impression that there is nothing wrong at all (and leading people to be surprised and angry when they make poor decisions). Others have very excellent mechanical, musical, or creative abilities. The problem is that their intelligence is often hampered by an unreliable short-term memory, difficulty holding more than one thing in their mind at a time, and trouble with "executive functions" such as getting organized, making good decisions, starting and wrapping up activities, and paying attention to the right thing at the right time. Their performance on academic and real-life tasks can vary from day to day, hour to hour. It can be very frustrating to be an intelligent person with

FASD! Not only does it feel like your brain has holes in it, but it also feels like the holes move around, and other people don't understand at all how or why things are so difficult.

3. FASD is rare. Diagnosis of FASD is relatively rare (Health Canada cites a prevalence rate of FASD in Canada of about 1%[9]) . but the effects of maternal alcohol use on developing brains are almost certainly more common. It is impossible to estimate the real prevalence of FASD, because of the social stigma attached to it. It takes a great deal of courage for a mother to admit that her child's problems might be caused by her drinking during pregnancy! No doubt many children with FASD, especially those who are living with their birth parents and are not under the care of social services, are diagnosed instead with one or more of these common problems: Learning Disabilities, ADHD, Autistic Spectrum Disorder, and Oppositional Defiant Disorder. This is not to suggest that all children with these disorders really have FASD in disguise; but some of them do. A child's situation (for example, being in care of the state), social class, and perceived race all may weigh in to the likelihood of being diagnosed with FASD.

4. People with FASD have no moral conscience, no empathy, or no ability to see the consequences of their actions. People with FASD are typically very empathic; they feel deeply with and for the people they love. They often have very strong emotions and are deeply and intuitively tuned in to others. They tend to be very loyal friends who will do anything for the ones they care about. Many develop especially strong bonds with animals. People with FASD are just as generous, just as kind, and just as loving as the rest of us. But they may make poor decisions in-the-moment

5. People with FASD become criminals. This is the myth with the strongest grain of truth to it, but it misses the mark by being too general and by confusing a criminal identity (i.e. getting caught) with criminal intentions, actions and personality.[10] People with

FASD are often easily led (remember the part about loyalty and wanting to help the people they care about?). Because they are often poor judges of character, and because their learning and behaviour differences make it hard for them to be accepted at school, they often gravitate toward people of poor character who lead them into foolish, risky, and even criminal behaviours. They may be further hampered by poor impulse control, a poor ability to consider the past, present and future at the same time while they make a decision in the here and now, and slow reaction time. That last point is important in determining who gets caught in a drug bust: the kid holding the bag is likely to be the kid with FASD.[11] For these reasons, people with FASD are greatly over-represented among prison populations.

6.   FASD is the cause of most problems among children in foster care and in late adoptions. Among children in care of the state or province, FASD comes hand in hand with relationship-based trauma and neglect. Malnutrition and other health problems may also complicate the mix. The longer a child is in unfavourable circumstances, the harder it is to form a good and firm relationship with an adoptive family. Having a nervous system that is compromised in its ability to link cause-and-effect, to think about past-present-future connections, or to find comfort when it is upset can make the job of connecting to a new family even harder. FASD and trauma complicate one another in a circular way, and it is impossible to tell where one picks up and the other leaves off.[12]

7.   Bad mothers are the cause of FASD. Blaming FASD on mothers is unfair and short-sighted. Firstly, much of the damage of alcohol exposure is done within the first two months of pregnancy; before most women know that they are pregnant.[13] Secondly, some of the women who are most in danger of giving birth to alcohol-affected babies are those who exist at the margins of society, are in unsupportive relationships, or suffer from their own traumas and tragedies. Many have FASD themselves. Drug

and alcohol treatment beds are scarce for women. Truly a society that is more supportive of girls and of women will produce fewer children with FASD. Finally, blaming mothers drives FASD into the shadows. This prevents good research, delays and prevents diagnosis and treatment, and keeps the negative stereotypes and stigmas intact. The "no shame, no blame" attitude is essential in approaching FASD in families; it's a challenge for us all to work on together.

8. Children with FASD will only break your heart. They might. Any child might break their parent's heart. And mend it, several times over a lifetime together. It's an unpredictable, challenging and rewarding journey, and the outcome can't possibly be predicted. What we can be fairly sure about is that these children benefit greatly from the love and support of dedicated parents. We also can be sure that the parents of these children need to have a great deal of information, supportive friends and family, tenacity, humour and courage. It's never easy, but it's sometimes wonderful.

Alcoholism, Family Stories and Heritage. Some groups of people have very high rates of alcoholism because they have experienced generations of hardship. Nana Rose, Oma Mika and Uncle Pete talk about how hardships sometimes bring on drinking and alcoholism.

Many adopted and foster children in Canada come from Aboriginal and First Nations heritage. In Canada, terrible epidemics swept through the communities of the First Nations just over 100 years ago. Those who survived were stunned and grieved deeply. But before they could rebuild their lives, the children were gathered away from their parents and sent to residential schools where they were not allowed to speak their languages, learn their people's ways, or worship in the ways of their parents and grandparents. Again, the death rate was high. This time it was children who were getting sick and dying, far from their homes.

By the time the last residential schools closed in the 1980's, many people thought that Canada's First Nations and Aboriginal Peoples would never recover. Rates of alcoholism and drug abuse were very high. Rates of FASD were also very high.

As I write this, Canada is engaged in a process called Truth And Reconciliation,[14] where Aboriginal and Caucasian people who attended and taught at the residential schools come together to share their stories, to mourn and to forgive. The cultures of Canada's Aboriginal Peoples reflect not only their old ways, but also new wisdom and strengths that come from facing the past and its heartaches. Aboriginal children are especially valued because they represent hope for a cultural and community renewal after so much collective loss and trauma. [15] If your children have Aboriginal heritage, you will certainly want to do more reading and talking with them about the good, and the hard things that happened to their ancestors.

Questions for the family about alcoholism, heritage and family histories:

- Why do you think Hunter got angry at Nana Rose's story? What made him change his mind and stop feeling so angry?

- Does your family serve or drink alcohol? What is the role that alcohol plays in your family?

- What is an alcoholic? How do you know if somebody is an alcoholic?

- Alcoholism tends to run in families, and some families have many members who have trouble with their drinking alcohol. This may be because some families have a genetic, inherited weakness that makes it easier for them to slide from drinking occasionally with friends to being addicted to alcohol. What does this mean for your adopted children?

- Is anybody in your family of Aboriginal or First Nations heritage?

- What happens to heritage when people get adopted?

- Should people keep the stories of their ancestors alive, even if those stories are sad? Even after adoption?

- What did Uncle Pete mean when he said that a circle was broken, because Hunter and Faith would do something different from their mother?

- Do you think that Hunter will keep his promise not to drink alcohol? Do you think that Faith will also decide this?

Chapter 11: Smashed Fingers

This chapter covers a lot of ground. We'll take one issue at a time.

Traumatic Memory

Faith has a "flashback" in this chapter; a memory that is more like a sensory experience than it is like a story. People who have had traumatic experiences often get this kind of memory, especially if they haven't had much opportunity to talk about the event.

When someone has a flashback, they usually don't actually see or hallucinate what has happened—that's the Hollywood version of a flashback. But their emotions come back very strongly, and often very suddenly, and the memory that they have may be of a sight, a pain, a sound, or even a smell; something very sensory. There is a sense of being there again, even though the person knows that they are not. People almost always have difficulty talking when they are having a flashback. The memory has become almost frozen in time, because the brain has remembered it only in sensations, not in words.Flashbacks are powerful experiences, and they may, at least for a few moments, take over whatever else is happening. Toni does the right thing to respond; she brings Faith close to her for comfort, speaks softly, and kisses Faith's fingers as if they were still hurting. This allows Faith to bring something new into the experience; kisses of comfort, and not being alone. Reaching out physically to Faith helps to break into the very private experience of flashback.

Here's what parents can do to help children deal with flashbacks:

- Offer physical contact. If the child doesn't easily tolerate being held yet, try wrapping him or her in a warm blanket.

- Warmth is important. The emotions of a flashback hit hard and change rapidly, often leading to a mild version of physiological shock. Tears, shaking and feeling chilly mean that the flashback itself is passing, and the body is striving to get back to a calm state. Offer a blanket or beach towel.

- Once the child is calming, ask him or her to "Name three things" that they can hear (right now), see, and touch.

- Let them cry; tears are a very healthy and natural reaction to rapid changes in emotion. In fact, when the tears come, the actual flashback is probably finished or passing, and the child has calmed down enough to let their guard down and have the tears flow. Reassure them that crying is fine.

- Help the child in a calmer state to put words to the story of what they remember. Pictures or toys may help with this; sometimes it is easier to show before telling. Drawing pictures together also slows down the experience of remember together, allowing more time for healing.

- Offer safety. Be clear and explicit about how things have changed and why they can expect to be safe now.

In the chapter Toni, Helen, Hunter and Faith all work to piece together what must have happened. When a traumatic memory finds its story in words, it can settle into the larger story of the person's life without having so much power to overtake and overwhelm. There is now a great deal of evidence from brain studies about how this works; getting the parts of the brain that register sensory information, emotion and words to work together is how the best psychotherapies work to heal or to reduce the impact of trauma on people's lives.[16]

Guilt, shame and regret

Meanwhile, Hunter has his own memory of the event, and it challenges him in quite a different way. Hunter feels caught, defensive and probably, deep down, ashamed of how he behaved when Faith was a baby. Will Toni and Helen be angry, he wonders. Hunter needs help to understand that he was too young at the time to understand and to take care of a baby.

When sisters or brothers are left to take care of younger siblings, it is very, very common that the younger siblings get mistreated in some way. Both the older and the younger children suffer. The older ones live with guilt and shame over things that they lacked the knowledge and/or the impulse control to prevent. The younger ones live with the feelings of betrayal and pain over having been mistreated by the very person they turned to for nurturance and protection.

Toni and Helen understand that both of the children were innocent. Hunter was in a situation that was too much for his small self, and Faith did what babies everywhere do. Toni and Helen show the children what forgiveness looks like by showing them equal love and affection. "No shame, no blame" is important in this story, as it is important in every aspect of raising adopted children.

Babies

Another thing that comes up in this chapter is babyhood. Children who are adopted after their babyhood is over may have missed out on the kinds of comfort and help that babies need. They may not have had enough of soaking up love and attention from people who found them adorable. Big kids often have complicated feelings toward babies—feelings of envy exist right alongside feelings of love and responsibility. For late adopted children, envy is perfectly normal and understandable. Likewise, it is understandable if some of our children don't like babies, don't like "feeling like a baby", or don't want to be around babies.

Some late-adopted children, on the other hand, love to pretend that they are babies, playing games like peek-a-boo and hide-and-seek (it's just a little more grown-up version of peek-a-boo, if you think about it …), rough-housing, riding on their parents' feet or piggy-back, wrapping up tight in a blanket, or even drinking from a bottle. Others are too self-conscious or feel too vulnerable with physical closeness to play at being babies. But there are still ways to offer a bit of healthy baby-like experiences. Here are some ways that adoptive families have managed to offer baby-like nurturance to older children who are uncomfortable with more obvious kinds of baby-play:

- Cuddling a child who is wrapped in a blanket or beach towel.

- Giving 'back hugs' from behind the child, rather than face-to-face.

- Letting the child 'catch' popcorn or small sweets (like M&M's) tossed a small distance by parents.

- Cooking together, and especially taste-testing as the parent holds the spoon,

- Offering a water bottle with a spout, especially during read-aloud times around bedtime.

- Playing string games and/or clapping games that pre-teen girls typically learn on the playground. There are books that teach string games, if you don't know any, and you may have to ask around to find some clapping games.

Questions for families to talk about:

About bad memories

What do you do when a bad memory hits? Do you try to think about something else, like changing the channel? Do you find something to comfort yourself, like a blanket, a bath, or something good to eat? Do you look for somebody who loves you to help by listening or by taking your mind off the bad thing?

About Regrets and Forgiveness

How does your family handle regrets?

What does it mean to forgive?

Should a person always forgive when they are treated badly? How do the parents in your family decide about forgiveness?

Perhaps someone in the family (maybe a parent) can tell a story about having messed up as a child, then finding forgiveness.

About Babies

Talk about a baby or two that you know. What do babies need?

How do babies communicate what they need?

Why do some people find babies hard to take care of?

Why do most people think that babies are sweet? Do you think that they are sweet?

Do you have pictures of when the children were babies and/or toddlers? If so, spend some time looking at these pictures, and talking about what you know, or what you would like to know, about when they were babies.

Chapter 12: Faith Strikes Out

Faith runs away!

Therapists say that children like Hunter and Faith have experienced Attachment-based trauma. Love itself has become strongly associated with feelings of pain, betrayal, and abandonment.[17] It's no wonder, then, that they seek to avoid going down that path again.

In this story, Hunter and Faith demonstrate two very different styles of dealing with this need to avoid loving feelings.

Hunter's style is to be well-behaved, quiet, and perhaps sneaky behind the backs of adults who try to love him. This sort of child may be praised by teachers and others as compliant, "never a problem", and polite. But parents may feel like there is a void behind the mask of good behaviour. Expressions of affection, if they come, are shallow and rote.

Adoptive parents typically have to wait many years before a child like Hunter shows them his real feelings. The positive side of this is that the waiting years are often calm, and the child may accomplish many skills and honours at school and elsewhere by showing how well they "know the ropes" of pleasing others. The negative side is the indifference of the child; it is painful to love a child who cannot return that affection. Nor does the calm always last; once in a while such a child may demonstrate their indifference through a breach of trust or a clear act of exploitation. At these times the whole family usually needs very skilled help as parents struggle to forgive what feels like betrayal on the part of a child who is still, after all, doing the best that they can do at being a family member.

Faith's style is to more openly challenge the parents for control of the family. This style of resistance comes to a head much more quickly than Hunter's mask of compliance. Open conflict is frequent, and it can be very challenging indeed for parents to resist reacting to the obvious face of defiance that confronts them.

Because this is fiction, Faith's rebellion is relatively mild and short-lived. The guidance of the ancestors is also an important factor in leading her back to the Greens. In real life, the Greens might be in for years of the children holding back, watching, testing, and periodically turning away, even running away from the love that they are offering.

People who adopt older children like Hunter and Faith live in hope, and in the knowledge that even if the outcome is not all that they dreamt of in their most optimistic moments, neither is any act of love wasted. Meanwhile, it is very important that they have strong sources of emotional and practical support for themselves to lean on.

Faith notices in the story that Helen is less reactive to the challenging behaviours of her and Hunter than she was at the beginning. Helen has learned to hold back instead of reacting. This is an important skill for people who parent children with attachment-based trauma. When calm is restored, the work of untangling the story begins.

Questions for the family:

Who in your family can understand the way that Faith is feeling? What emotion-words (like happy, sad, angry, worried, confused, etc.—words that name a feeling rather than a thought) might describe Faith's feelings at the beginning, the middle, and the end of the chapter?

Who in your family can understand the way that Hunter is feeling? What emotion-words might describe his feelings about the Greens? About Faith?

How do you think Hunter feels at the end of the day when they are all back together?

How do you think Helen and Toni feel?

Do you think that Faith will try running away again? Why or why not?

Chapter 13: the BS-ometer

Probably every parent who ever lived has wanted to count on the truth of words that came out of their children's mouths. As the ancestors would say, mutual trust is the very bedrock of close relationships. However, in the adoptive family, words can seldom be counted upon to be truthful. In families where lying is common and automatic, trust has to be built in different ways.

Parents contribute to trust in the family by providing trustworthy care. They must also be willing to repair the relationship, again and again, after misunderstandings and hurt. Parents must also be scrupulously honest.

The children will gradually learn to be trustworthy. Loyalty under fire and generosity may come long before reliable truthfulness from late-adopted children. It is exhausting and exasperating, but being lied to is inevitable. As the parents it is especially important not to confuse blind trust with love or loyalty, and to repeat often, "my faith in the truthfulness of your words has nothing to do with my faith that you are loveable and worthy of my commitment." To love is not necessarily to believe without question.

Late-adopted children lie for many reasons; some that they share with more typical children in intact families, and some that are more unique to children who have experienced attachment-based trauma.

Reasons that children lie include:

- Not wanting to "get in trouble". This is actually two reasons: a) not wanting to be punished, and b) not wanting to feel the shame of having messed up.

- Wanting to look good and impress people.

- Wanting to manipulate another person into doing something. This sounds bad, but wanting to have power is the healthy root of creativity and learning. Learning how and why to go for positive expressions of personal power, and to resist manipulative, untrue, destructive or unfair expressions of power over others takes time and patience.

- Wanting to have some private secrets that parents do not share. This is much more common in foster and late-adopted children, and it is a way of resisting too much closeness when the child does not feel safe and ready to relax their guard.

How should parents respond to lying? It is probably best to:

- Avoid over-reacting in a judgemental and punitive way. This is harder than it sounds.

- Do correct obvious falsehoods. Try to do so in a matter-of-fact way that does not shame.

- If a child lies often, develop a way to signal when she or he has lost their credibility and is veering off into clear falsehoods. In our family, the BS-ometer was invented for this very purpose. It's an imaginary instrument that elicits a "beep, beep, beep" sound when someone is detecting a lie.

- Sometimes you will probably think that your child has lied when actually they are telling the truth. Don't sweat this over-much. Not believing someone is not the same thing as not loving them. If a child often lies, then a logical consequence is that people may not believe them when they tell the truth. Remember the story of the child who cried wolf? It's a good one to tell again.

- Notice and acknowledge, quietly and in a way that protects the child's pride and dignity, when they are becoming more truthful or when they tell a difficult truth. Point out how courageous it is to tell the truth.

- Don't tell lies to children, or in front of children. Be trust-worthy.

Questions for the family:

Have you ever told a lie? Tell a story about a time when you lied, how the truth came out (if it did), and what happened because of it. Make this a light story, and give it a comic touch if possible.

What does it mean that "Lies break trust"?

How does a person build trust back after telling a lie?

If someone doesn't believe what you are saying, does that mean that they don't like you?

What is blind faith? (It's believing everything you are told). What is the difference between being loyal to someone, and having blind faith in what they say?

What does Uncle Pete mean by "Keep your eyes open"? What are some things that each member of your family wants the others to see when they "keep their eyes open" and judge for themselves what is good and true?

Chapter 14: That Touch Thing

Hunter doesn't like being touched. There could be several reasons for this. As a pre-teen boy, he may be on the brink of developmental changes that make him uncomfortable within his body, and uncomfortable with any affectionate touch from mothers. He is also receiving cultural messages about boys, masculinity, touch and mothers that may lead him to react negatively to a motherly touch. Such a touch may threaten his emerging sense of himself as masculine. These would be fairly typical reasons behind a pre-teen boy's discomfort with motherly displays of physical affection.

But for Hunter, and for many older adopted children, the developmental reasons for wanting less touch mix with reasons that are based in Attachment Trauma and in resisting attachment itself. Hunter doesn't want to feel vulnerable. In fact, Hunter doesn't want to feel anything toward Helen and Toni. He wants to hold out and to keep his emotional independence, which he imagines will shelter him from further harm.

He is both right and wrong, of course. Loving feelings do at times make a child vulnerable. Once they have been moved a certain number of times (and how many times varies by child), foster children usually become very guarded about love. At the same time, Hunter is missing out on the opportunity to have relationships that could help him to develop emotional strength and stability at a much deeper level. It is sad, and also frustrating for parents to watch a child hold out for emotional independence rather than submit to being treasured and loved.

Hunter's aversion to touch may also come, in part, from having been abused physically or interfered with sexually. When trust is violated so profoundly it is very, very difficult to receive touch, let alone to enjoy it.

Some children are averse to touch because it overloads their sensitive nervous systems. This experience of sensory overload is especially common among children with FASD.[18]

Yet Toni and Helen persist in offering touch to Hunter. To them, touch represents comfort as well as emotional closeness. They understand the positive power of touch. Even Uncle Pete agrees that Hunter needs to expand his capacity to give and to receive touch within the family circle. Touch is one of the gifts of having a real, "forever" family. It is also one of the things that feels good and rewarding to parents. It is important to have some good and rewarding experiences woven into this job of parenting tough kids—parents are in danger of burning out if they don't get back some of the affection that they put out to these children.

Some strategies that foster and adoptive parents we know have used to get past the touch barrier include:

- Massaging the children's feet or hands. These parts, being farthest away from the vulnerable body core, are often "safer" feeling places to start in receiving touch.

- Rough-housing. Use caution with this. Many children who have been in state or provincial care do not have an "off" button for rough-housing, and will escalate the energy level until someone gets hurt or something gets broken. Keep rough-housing to a defined area, for a defined amount of time, and with clearly agreed upon "stop now" signals. Never tickle or rough-house a child who is saying "stop!", and don't allow siblings to over-ride a "stop" signal, either.

- Blankets and quilts. These can form just the right degree of barrier between two bodies as to make the cuddle or hug feel "safe". They can also bundle a child up like a sausage, creating a safe, snuggled feeling without the emotional risk of direct contact.

- Back hugs. Hugging a child from behind with their back against your front is usually easier for the child than face-to-face, which is more intense. One caveat—don't surprise them with a back hug. But do be aware of when a child is "backing in to hug position", and respond appropriately.

- Controlled contact and balancing games and stunts, like the classic "airplane" pose: the child is balanced in the air as the parent, back to the floor, holds him or her on raised feet and hands.

Be creative. Many short, small touches per day are easier and more effective than a few big ones. Reach out for a pat on the shoulder or a hand on the arm frequently.

Ask, "what feels ok to you? What is especially hard?"

Recognize and tactfully praise the courage it takes to accept loving touch. Express your appreciation for being allowed to touch your touch-phobic child.

Family questions:

How does each family member like best to be touched? How do they like least to be touched?

Is it okay to tickle someone without asking first in your family? How about rubbing hair, or shoulders? How about a hug?

How do you say "stop" when you don't like the way someone is touching you?

Who is the "touchiest" person in the family—the one that likes cuddles and touch the most? Who is the least touchy?

Some kids like to rough-house with tackles and wrestling. How does your family deal with this?

Some kids love to touch their dogs, cats or stuffies. Does anybody in your family like to cuddle non-human friends?

Chapter 15: Hunter On His Own?

Hunter meets Nathan, a boy who is living independently at 17. Nathan, like most who "age out" in the care of the state or province, is not thriving or making a smooth transition from childhood to becoming an independent adult. Spotty education, poor life skills, and the absence of a stable family home to turn to during the back-and-forth transition into adulthood all add up to high risk for poverty, homelessness and substandard housing, and repetition of the addictions and problems of the parent generation.[19]

In Nathan, Hunter gets a view of what "might have been", and the romanticism of living on his own becomes less attractive.

At what age do children expect to live on their own? Late adoptees may have stories from their first families about leaving home in the early teenage years. In our part of the world, it isn't uncommon to hear of children leaving home at 16, sometimes to live at the house of an accommodating friend. Yet these expectations are out of sync with the realities of life in the 21st century. A high school diploma is not the ticket to adulthood that it was 30 years ago. In Canada, it is typical for people to live at home with their parents, and/or to move in and out several times until the mid-20's.[20] The stability of a place to land in the early and mid-20's is one of the greatest potential advantages of being adopted vs. growing up in foster care.

The urge to be independent can be very strong among late-adopted teens, and some do run away, go into foster care, or even return to biological family during their teens. These are high-risk years for estrangement between adoptive parents and their children. The heart-break of adoption disruption is terrible on both sides. There is a great need for research to explore what works and what does not in terms of support for adoptive parents, contact with birth families, and supports for teens in adoption and foster care during these key years.

Long-time foster and adoptive parents tell us that most, but not all late-adopted children make the adopted family their own, permanently. We have a long way to go in learning how to promote stability in adoptions while allowing teens and young adults to build their sense of iden-tity—with all of its biological, social and cultural elements.

Family questions:

What do you think is a good age for people to move out on their own from their parents' home? Why?

What needs to be in place in a person's life before they are ready to live on their own? What skills should a person have? Is a job necessary? Is there such a thing as leaving home too soon? As waiting too long?

How do parents help when it is time to move out and live on your own?

What in-between options will your family have when teens become young adults and want more independence?

Chapter 16: Thinking It Over

The ice is broken, and Hunter talks things over with Helen and Toni. No more secrets? We hope so. In a real adoptive family, things might go back-and-forth a few more times between keeping secrets and talking.

Adoptive children can be awfully silent about what is on their minds sometimes. Finding the words is hard, and finding the trust is also hard. It would be lovely to have some funny and wise ancestor-ghosts around to help bridge the gap.

At this point in the story, we were wondering what advice the ancestors might give to Toni and Helen. Of course, grown-ups almost never see ghosts—not in real life, and not in stories. But they do often have the experience of seeing people in their dreams who have already died. This could happen to Helen with her father, for instance. And who is to say that the people we meet in dreams aren't ancestors trying to teach us, at least sometimes?

At the end of the chapter, the two parents and Hunter are looking for candles to light while they remember their loved ones in prayers. Prayers are one way that families can remember their loved ones. They are also a way of unloading some of the worry over loved ones that have bad troubles like drug or alcohol addictions. Even if your family is not religious, it helps to develop some kind of ritual for remembering, honouring, and letting the worry go to some greater power. Many people use candles; some throw stones into the ocean or write names in the sand when the tide is coming in. These are loving things to do when reaching out directly is impossible or unwise.

Family questions:

If you were the ancestors, what would you want to explain to Toni and Helen about Faith and Hunter? What do parents need to know?

What do you think about Toni, Helen and Hunter praying together?

How does your family show its love for people who have died, or who live apart?

Chapter 17: Shadow Boxing

Uh-oh. Every set of parents has doubts sometimes about what they have done to their pre-parenting life. But it's never something that they want their children to overhear!

Toni and Helen have a crisis of confidence, and it takes Hunter only a small exposure to their doubt to convince him that it is time to move on.

This vulnerability of faith is expected at the beginning of older child adoption, and for some children it lasts for years.

Once again the ancestors help out with something that isn't available in real life—the ability to "replay" the whole situation and see what really happened.

This chapter is here to help children know that a bad day does not signal the end of an adoptive parent's commitment. It is also here for the parents in the family—to let parents know that they are not alone, and it is common to lose heart. We do, however, carry on, living in hope and seeking out new ideas and sources of support.

It is a definite advantage when adoptive parents have close family and friends to help out, and to listen and encourage when things are going rough. Parenting was never meant to be done in isolation. Most of human history has been lived in communities where rubbing shoulders with other parents happened many times a day—gathering water, milling or pounding grain, and baking bread in a common oven still brings women together in a few very rural places. Children in these places may be poor by the standards of modernized countries, but there are advantages, too, from growing up as part of a watchful village. They have many "aunties" and "uncles" to teach them (like the ancestors!), and unless war interrupts their life they rarely have the kind of dramatic experiences of trauma, rescue and adoption by strangers that Faith and Hunter experienced.

How can we re-create a healthy "village" for our adopted children— where there are many trustworthy adults for parents and children to turn to in times of hardship and trouble? Helen and Toni talk about reaching out to other parents and to professional help. Yet full time careers take a toll on the community of parents.

School activities and organized activities like sports provide a starting place for new adoptive parents to join the community of parents in general. Parents of typically developing children may not automatically understand the quirks of raising children with attachment traumas and the other problems that come with the Older Adoptive Child experience. But the kind ones are always open to learn, and to lend an encouraging comment. Some will even offer respite in the form of a play date—a double gift of "time off" for mom and friendship for both mother and child. The parents of older adopted children missed the stage of bonding with other parents over first steps and baby teeth, but they can still step into the community of parents and make allies.

Parents of older adopted children also need one another. There are many experiences and feelings that are unique to this journey, and it is immensely comforting to hear someone else say, "I've been there, too."

There is also a very big place in the community for professionals who specialize in working with older adoptees and their parents. Methods of child and family therapy that are effective with "normal" families can fall flat, or even be harmful, with adoptees. Therapists who work alone with older child adoptees can develop an attachment-like relationship that competes with and undermines the one with adopted parents. This is so easy to do because attachment-traumatized children actually prefer the no-strings-attached form of intimacy offered by a therapist over the "pick-up-your-socks-and-I-know-your-dark-side" complexity of having real parents. Therapists themselves often grew up dreaming about helping children, and the lure of a child who seems to love you more than they love the parents that they live with is very strong. The first job of a therapist working with adopted children is to strengthen the tested and frayed string of attachment that holds them to their adopted parents.

Providing therapeutic services to adopted families is an area for specialized training. Adoptive parents should look for a therapist who has the training and background to help.[21]

Chapter 18: Social Worker

This was Serena's favorite chapter to write, and our children's favourite one to hear. It is a happy chapter, where the children and their new family make it through a crisis and come out stronger.

Calling the social worker is one way that many foster children get moved on to their next home. In an ideal world, the social worker would have a magic crystal ball for investigating the complaints of children, and of other people who might be watching a family. With a magic crystal ball, they would never make the mistake of leaving children where the danger is real; and they would also never take children away from a home where it was possible to work things out and stay. Stability may not always be what children want at every moment, but it is very important for them in the long run!

Unfortunately, social workers have no magical crystal ball. They rely on the words of children to make decisions that will shape lives, for better or for worse. They rely upon their own best judgement, too. Some may have prejudices that interfere with their being able to see things clearly. And the systems that they work within and the tools that they have to work with are very limited indeed (when compared, for instance with the magic and wisdom of the ancestors!).

Some of the most maligned social workers are in the field of Child Protection. These people get all of the blame for breaking up families that maybe could have stayed together if circumstances had been better and support services had been more available. On the other hand, they are rarely thanked when they make a child's life safer or better by removing them from danger or neglect. It takes a very special person to choose social work as a profession.

Mary, like most social workers that we know, is not popular with the children. I apologize to any social workers who are reading this book and who might feel hurt by the portrayal of Mary as a busy-body who needs special handling by the children. On the other hand, anybody who is studying to be a social worker should be for-warned; the children involved might not like you, even if you buy them treats.

Your family might follow up this chapter with stories of social workers—good, bad, and just human—that they have known. Or you might just want to talk about a time in your family life that started out as a crisis but made you stronger in the end.

Family questions:

What is the job of a social worker?

What qualities do you think make a good social worker? A not-so-good one?

Mary seems to be concerned about the children being raised by two women who are married to each other. What do you think about this family arrangement?

What makes you feel proud about the family you have?

What makes your family strong?

Would you have the courage that Faith and Hunter have to stand up for your family? What would it feel like to do that?

Chapter 19: December Meltdown

December is a high-stress month for families! This is especially true when families have gone through a big change, like adoption, the year before. The tension builds—will Christmas happen in this new family? Can the parents pull it off? Expectations can balloon, leading to giant balloon-sized disappointments. By the end of this chapter Faith is on the verge of a full-fledged meltdown.

Obviously, this family needed to do some better communicating about the Christmas season and expectations!

A rather nice thing that happens in this chapter is that Faith and Hunter start some Christmas preparations of their own. Children in foster care often have very little experience with initiating good things on their own. They get used to waiting to see what the adults will do. Faith and Hunter making Christmas decorations shows that they are starting to feel like this is their home, and that making the family work is their job, too.

Family questions:

What are your family holiday traditions?

How have your children celebrated Christmas in past years?

Have each person say one thing that they wish about December.

Have each person say one thing about December that they hope won't happen.

How do the adults in your family divide up the extra chores and activities that happen in December?

Do the parents in your family have extra work duties in December? Many do: teachers and store clerks typically have to put in many extra hours in December, just when children and partners most miss them at home. How does your family deal with this pressure?

Chapter 20: Christmas Preparations

Helen and Toni are over their heads. Fortunately, they are not alone. Helen and Toni discover two sources of help that can bring the some of the longed-for Christmas magic to the family: the children themselves, and community activities.

Here are some tips for making December easier in a changing family:

1. Borrow Christmas spirit from community events. Not all of the decorating and beauty has to happen at home. Craft markets are usually awash with music and good cheer, and are quite a bit less commercial than going to the shopping mall.

2. Taking in community events has a few special challenges for late-adopted children and their parents. Getting separated and lost in the crowd happens quickly when you don't have the "invisible rubber bands" of well-formed attachment between parents and children. Make sure you review the rules for staying together, and have a rallying point established as soon as you arrive.

3. If your family happens to be Christian, then December (Advent) is also a very important religious season, and going to church often lends moments of quiet wonder to balance out the mayhem. Other faiths also have celebrations in mid-winter with lights, stories, food and song—there seems to be a near-universal need among people of the Northern Hemisphere to gather and brighten December this way. Taking in some of these traditions as a guest may take some of the load off parents to be "on" as the one source of Christmas for children.

4. Get outdoors! We combine a walk outdoors with wreath-making indoors; a very easy craft that always turns out beautiful.

5. Watch the sweets! Pack along some cheese and crackers to balance out the extra sugar, and, if at all possible, influence event planners not to over-do the sweet offerings. The ups and downs of blood sugar in the pre-Christmas season add significantly to emotional over-reactivity.

6. Give children short, simple directions ("put on your red sweater with the snowflake.") Add time limits (a visible timer is great) and incentives to pace the action.

7. Practice "tag team parenting" to keep up with the paid work (which, in so many occupations, comes thick and fast in December) and so that each gets some quiet breaks.

8. Set priorities and stick to them. Don't try to do everything.

9. Prepare children in the evening for what is happening the day before. Minimize surprises.

The build-up of toys in children's rooms is a modern-day challenge. Our great-grandparents had only a few toys at most; today's children have to sort and pare down toys on a regular basis. This is not such a bad thing; it gives them very good practice at facing what they most treasure, and at letting go of stuff that isn't important anymore. What a terrific life skill! It's a bit much for Faith to handle, and the truth is that it is over the heads of most eight-year-olds. It may be especially hard for children who have had many losses and/or traumas in their lives. Some want to hold on to absolutely everything; others are too ready to let go of treasures carelessly. Helen and Toni were probably foolish to leave this to the last minute: November would have been a better month.

Family questions:

Faith and Hunter come up with some good ideas for things they, themselves, can do while they wait for Helen and Toni to get the Christmas tree up. What would the children in your family like to do?

Does your family have a stash of craft supplies that children can access independently to make decorations or gifts?

Are there family friends who would pitch in by taking the children for part of a day to make crafts or do holiday baking? This can be a good time to "share the children" around among people who miss and need some child energy in their lives.

What are your family's must-do priorities for the Holiday season? What expectations might be dropped? How will you plan and work ahead for the must-do things to happen?

How does your family handle gift-shopping or gift-making? Do the children get a special 'Christmas gift buying' allowance? Do they make crafts for special people? You may want to talk about adult Christmas shopping, too. How much is typically spent on Christmas in your family? What kinds of gifts do people get? (This is an area of great interest and some worry for children who are new to the family. Talking about it in a matter-of-fact way reduces the surprise element, and the nervous tension that goes with it.)

What happens in your family when a parent has a meltdown (cries, yells, or otherwise shows that they are over their heads)?

How do you know when you have too many toys, or clothes, or just too much stuff? What do you do about it?

Chapter 21: Everything Changes

With every adoption, there are losses as well as gains to the families involved. Bringing together old and new families is much, much harder than it sounds. Different styles and values between families, resentments between the family that 'lost' its children and the family that 'gained' them, children's divided loyalties and confusion over who to love as 'real' parents, and the capacity of children "divide and conquer" are just some of the challenges that are built in to the relationship between old and new parents.

Every family has its own style and culture, from what it eats for breakfast to how it deals with the big questions of meaning and spirituality. Biological, foster and adoptive parents will sometimes, but not always, be able to bridge the family culture gap with tact and appreciation. Diversity can be a source of strength for the children; divided loyalties a source of weakness.

Would you choose your child's biological parent as a friend if you met by chance? It is a rare exception to find natural, unstrained friendships between biological and adoptive parents. But they can treat one another with courtesy and respect—this should always be the case.

Regular contact with birth families is not always in the best interests of the children. Active drug or alcohol addictions sometimes still haunt the birth families of children who are adopted late. Adoptive parents may feel anger toward the birth parents if the child was abused or neglected before coming into state care. Birth parents, on the other hand, may not appreciate the generosity of adoptive parents. A few cannot get past seeing adoptive parents as usurpers who selfishly keep children that are not their own. It is much easier to speak respectfully of such birth families from a safe distance than when they are actively interfering with a child's attachment to the new parents. If these dynamics are present, professional help should be sought and contact should wait until the child is an adult.

If you opt for ongoing contact, be prepared for some confusion and even rebellion in the teen years. Two active sets of parents will frustrate and confuse children. They will often feel very strongly about who the "real parents" are, and actively reject and distance themselves from the other. But as absolute as these allegiances are one day, they may change the next. A conflict with adoptive parents may bring out the dreaded, "You aren't my real mom!", or, much more serious, a secret attempt to contact and complain to the lost biological parent.

Old and new families need to keep a united front, and the adoptive parents need to be in the lead. If there are divisions, the child will learn to exploit them. This isn't because they are being bad; it's because it is every child's job to find and to use the sources of power that are available—even manipulative power. It does, however, need to be "nipped in the bud". Manipulating others by feeding conflict isn't ethical.

Sometimes, adoptive families will connect more easily with a grandparent or other adult in the birth parent's family. This is one way for children to have some connection with their biological and cultural heritage which minimizes some of the problems inherent in birth parent-adoptive parent dynamics—provided the grandparent is ready to truly accept the full legitimacy and authority of the adoptive parents.

Among advocates of open adoption there is a naive tendency to see "openness" as all-good; a panacea against the painful outcomes of adoptions in past decades. But this has very little research backing it; open adoption in the modern context is, with the possible exception of First Nations cultures, a new idea. There are certainly risks as well as benefits, and we look forward to some sound research which would allow "best practice" protocols to be developed.

Meanwhile, our knowledge of child development, family life, and attachment suggests that openness be:

- Maintained for people that the children have had a positive attachment-style relationship with.Kept at a level that does not impose undue levels of extra work and stress for adoptive parents.

- Arranged to allow children to experience their adoptive family as the "real" one that comes first at special times. If previous family members are to share in Christmas, Birthdays, or other special events, it should be very clear that they are invited guests of the adoptive family.

- Always under the watchful eye of adoptive parents, until the child is old enough leave home and/or to make consistently safe decisions with regard to relationships.

- Respectful to the adoptive parents as "real" parents, whose commitment to the children is as great as if they had been born to them, and who need the children's faith and confidence in order to fulfill this commitment.

The Martins in this chapter model exactly the compassion, respect and love that we hope for every child who has to make the transition from one family to another. They show that expanding "family" to include emotionally healthy members of the child's emotional family from before the adoption has great benefits for the children.

Why bother with openness in adoption? Openness is, at its core, resistance to the idea of cut-off that once formed the bedrock of adoption practices. Cut-offs are traumatic and leave a wound that is prone to reopen whenever the child feels stressed and unloved in the future. Cut-offs can be family time-bombs, ready to go off with devastating consequences at some future time when a dreamed-for reunion becomes possible.

Openness allows for relationships to develop and change naturally over time, but it does not guarantee a no-pain adoption. All of the adults need to be mature enough to handle conflicting emotions and to put the children's needs for security, clarity and faith in their new families above personal pride. They need to be ready to take their own desire to be nurtured and recognized elsewhere, rather than counting on children to fill the gaps within. They need the impulse control to hold their tongues over minor disagreements, keeping in mind the larger picture of giving the children a permanent family to grow in and to believe in.

Family questions:

Who would your children invite, if they could, to a special family dinner? Why?

Is there anyone that they would not invite, if the choice was theirs to make? Why?

Why do some people call biological parents "real parents"? How does that make you feel?

Draw a family chart, with stick figures (or drawings), circles and lines to show the immediate family (the current, adoptive family), the birth family (usually in a separate circle), and important extended family members such as grandparents, aunts and uncles, and cousins. Include in other circles important foster families. Use big paper! Talk about how they moved from one circle to the next. Use the chart to show boundaries.

Chapter 22: Christmas

It comes at last! The first Christmas in the adoptive home is a milestone. Even in homes that don't celebrate Christmas, the 25th of December will be a very important time. For the children, this is an important 'test' of the new family—will there be presents? Will the parents keep their promises, including promises of limits (in this story, 'no electronics')? Will there be alcohol served, and will it be allowed to ruin the day? Will there be fights, tears, curses, or broken things?

The first Christmas should be a calm one, with a minimum of visitors and modest gifts. Too much excitement is over the ability of most late-adopted children to handle. They need calm, quiet times in the day to balance the excitement of gifts and visitors. They need a balance of go-ahead treats (in this story, the stockings are a go-ahead) and delayed gratification (opening gifts with the family). The food should include a good balance of protein and complex carbohydrates with the sweets.

Once the mayhem of December is over, many families find the week or two between Christmas and the restart of school to be a magical time. Not until summer will most families have another week-long stretch of together-time. Pay attention during these times to the signs of attachments forming and trust growing. They may be subtle, but watch for:

- The emergence of calm contentment as an emotional state.

- Better acceptance of affectionate touch; perhaps even children seeking out touch from parents or sitting close together.

- Accepting comfort from parents when feeling blue, sick or in pain.

- Children wanting parents to "Look!" at what they are doing, or what they are looking at.

- Acceptance and appreciation of the food that parents make.

- Wanting to sleep in one room.

Hunter and Faith feel the unexpected emergence of joy. They also the feel echoes of anxiety from a time when they could not know what "safe" felt like. The absence of anxiety and the emergence of gentle, positive emotions indicate a state of Peace in the home. This may be very unfamiliar to the children, and hard to detect or describe at first. It may even set off a counter-reaction of chaos, as a child unfamiliar with Peace seeks to "stir things up" to a more familiar energy.

We use the image of a tiny bird to describe Peace in the home. It is a little bird that can't stay where there is too much fear, anxiety, or distress between people. But if we are at peace with one another, the little bird settles down among us, invisible but comfortable enough to stay a while. We put up a small symbol of Peace in the home—an ornament borrowed from the Christmas box. Hung where everyone can see, this ornament represents the Peace bird. If anyone in the family feels that Peace has left the house, they can take and hide the Peace bird. This is our signal that we need to find out what the problem is and handle it in such a way that the bird will come back. The symbolic Peace Bird helps to make that invisible quality of Peacefulness more visible, and it teaches children that each person holds the power to influence the Peacefulness of a home.

Family questions:

What emotions do Hunter and Faith experience in this chapter?

How do you know when you are feeling joyful? Anxious? (Focus on body sensations that go with these emotions.)

What is your favourite way to bring feelings of peacefulness or joy into your body? Into your home?

How do you like to spend family time?

What does your family do for family time that you want to do someday with your own children?

Do you think that the children were disappointed that they didn't get more things for Christmas?

Chapter 23: Lighting Candles

We all belong; we just don't always know it. If we could see beneath the surface of things, we would see that we are connected:In nature, through the water that circulates through our bodies as it travels just one small part of its larger journey—down as rain, nourishing plants and animals, gathering in rivers, streams and lakes, joining the oceans where it travels the great currents and up again as part of the atmosphere.

- Through the air we breath—the same air that every living thing before us, every animal and every ancestor, breathed before us.

- Through the genetic lines, the loves and the births that brought us here as our singular, unique selves.

- Through the lines of love and nurturance, generation after generation, that created and passed on traditions and knowledge about how to live.

- Through the lines of history that shaped the lives of our people through hardships and losses, strengths and healing triumphs.

In this chapter, Attachment is finally explained directly to the children (and to the readers). Adoptive parents know about Attachment; often they have read and talked a great deal about it. But spelling it out to the children helps to enroll them directly in the project. By the end of the story, Hunter and Faith are able to understand and accept the challenge of actively fostering feelings of Attachment toward their adoptive parents.

Attachment makes parenting easier. It makes children feel like watching for where their parents are (rather than darting off in all directions or out-of-view), feel like taking leadership and doing what they are asked to do, feel like asking directly and simply for what they need, and feel better inside when their parents are nearby. It makes adults feel powerful and special, almost magical, in their ability to be what their children need. Parenting attached children is richly rewarding, because they return our efforts with happy, warm gazes, laughter, growth and visible signs of thriving.

Waiting for Attachment to develop can be excruciating. There may be years (yes, years, and they will feel like decades) when our loving looks meet cold shoulders, our attempts to embrace are shrugged away, and our kind words seem to bounce off the children like rubber balls against a brick wall. This is acutely painful. It resonates as rejection in the parts of our brain where our own feelings of Attachment (safety, comfort, courage, and openness to learn) lie, alongside our deepest fears—that no one will love us, that we are unworthy of love, that we will be left alone. We may suffer from what psychologist Dan Hughes calls Blocked Care: the inability to keep feeling that love that once swelled within us at the sight of our adopted child.

Have courage. You are not alone. Your love is not wasted. You, like the children, belong.

Family questions:

Who are your ancestors?

How do you imagine your grandchildren will talk about you?

What traditions do you want to hand down to your children, and to their children?

What do you think about the Four Pillars of Attachment? Would you like to make something in your home to remind you of them?

How are you doing with each of the Four Pillars? It might be useful now and then to do a "Four Pillars Check-up", where each family member rates the family on a 1 - 10 scale on each quality: Safety, Comfort, Encouragement (or Courage to Explore) and Learning. Remember, building Attachment is a process, and keeping Attachments healthy is a lifelong practice.

(Endnotes)

1. Psychologist Daniel Siegel has written a great deal about the developing brains of children, and about parenting in a manner that is attuned to this brain development. A good place to start is his parenting book , *The Whole Brain Child*, published in 2011 by Delacourt Press.

2. We have learned a great deal from Psychologist Daniel Hughes, who has dedicated his career to helping families with late-adopted children experience healthy relationships of attachment. All families can benefit from his works, including *Attachment-Focused Parenting*, (published in 2009 by Norton) where he introduces the PACE model.

3. The cornerstone work for understanding the development of shame and guilt in children is Erik Erikson's *Childhood and Society*, first published in the 1950's. His theory was elegantly re-stated near the end of his life in *The Life Cycle Completed: a review*. Erikson noted that shame is the social feeling of being seen in one's inferiority or inadequacy; the remedy to shame is to hide or turn away from the judgement of others. Shame motivates lying, lashing out, blaming others, and hiding. Guilt is a feeling of responsibility, which implies the ability to do better or to repair what has been broken. Guilt motivates making amends and reparations. Guilt is more mature, and emerges later than shame (if it emerges at all). Children who have been mistreated or abandoned early in their lives have a much heightened sense of shame. This heightened sense of shame can block or delay the

self-awareness and responsibility that leads to the more mature emotions of guilt.

4.   Daniel Hughe's book, *Building the Bonds of Attachment: Awakening Love in Deeply Troubled Children*, (2nd edition, published in 2006 by Jason Aronson) gives a lovely illustration of rage and shame giving way to vulnerability and grief in an attachment-traumatized child. This is becoming a "classic" for foster and adoptive parents, and for the therapists who work with these families.

5.   Another important resource is the work of Pediatric Neuro-Psychiatrist Bruce Perry, whose website is listed below, and whose books provide a wonderfully readable introduction to the interplay of trauma and brain development.

6.   Attachment is the psychologist's word for the unique kind of love that a child holds for their primary caregiver(s); the people whom they rely upon for care, comfort, safety, and leadership from infancy onward. It is the key to everything, and we will speak much more about it as we go.

7.   Meg Hickling has several excellent resources for children and parents, including *The New Speaking of Sex: What your children need to know and when they need to know it*, Northstone Publishing, 2005, and *Boys, Girls and Body Science: a first book about the facts of life*, Harbour Publishing, 2002. *Boys, Girls and Body Science* is very informative yet giggle-worthy, suitable for parents to read aloud with children from approximately the age of 7 or 8 to teens.

8.   This study was first reported by DeLoache and Brown in 1979, and remains one of our favorite stories of developmental research (see Works Cited).

9.   Researchers at the University of British Columbia have been studying the impact of maternal alcohol use on the epigenome: the molecular "tags" attached to DNA sequences that influence

varied and differentiated expressions of the same genotype in different individuals. The work of Joanne Weinburg and her associates is demonstrating that the impact of maternal (and paternal) alcohol use upon pre-natal development is more complex and subtle than once thought. The work of the researchers is fascinating, but a difficult read for most parents. Physician Rod Densmore's collection of lectures and resources packaged in his book and CD set *FASD Relationships* gives a layperson's account of this research, and much more. (see Works Cited)

10. Occupational Therapist Diana Malbin has been a strong advocate for people with FASD, especially in the school system. She is one of several excellent educators who have contributed to this list of FASD symptoms and features. See Works Cited for her book.

11. CanFASD website: www.canfasd.ca/research-teams/prevalence. A recent study of the prevalence of FAS (full Fetal Alcohol Syndrome) and FASD (the more inclusive Fetal Alcohol Spectrum Disorder) among children and youth in the care of child welfare systems (foster care, orphanages, and other public residential child care) estimated that 6% of the children met the full diagnostic criteria for FAS, and 16.9% for FASD (Lange, Shield, Rehm 7 Popova, 2013).

12. The John Howard Society of Ontario has produced an excellent fact sheet on FASD and imprisonment. See Works Cited.

13. This insight into "who gets caught holding the bag" comes from Kee Warner of the White Crow Village FASD Society. White Crow Village holds week-long family education camps that combine the traditional joys of camp for kids with intensive education for parents. See their programs and materials at www.whitecrowvillage.org

14. Physician and parent of a child with FASD, Rod Densmore has much to say about this intersection of risk: FASD and early relationship trauma. In his book, *FASD Relationships*, he cites and

builds upon the work of Psychologist and Attachment Educator Gordon Neufeld, showing how the tasks and processes that are necessary and expectable for child-to-parent attachment become challenged not only by early trauma but by the nature of FASD as brain damage. A nervous system that does not integrate sensory information well, regulate its emotional states well, or think simultaneously about multiple points in time well presents serious challenges to a child who is trying to gain a sense of safety and continuity in relationship to a new parent.

15. Phillip Haycock summarized recent and historical research on the effects of pre-pregnancy and early pregnancy alcohol exposure on fetal development in an interesting but fairly technical article in the ejournal *Biology of Reproduction.* See Works Cited.

16. The Truth and Reconcilliation Commission of Canada continues to produce news and resources on Aboriginal history and healing. There are many moving stories and resources accessible through the TRC website: www.trc.ca

17. If you have an Aboriginal teen, we recommend Monique Gray Smith's wonderful story *Tilly. Tilly* combines a good story with much teaching about the traditions, wisdom, history and faith of Aboriginal peoples.

18. John Briere is one of the top researchers and therapists in the world today working with childhood trauma and therapy. His latest textbook, *Principles of Trauma Therapy,* is a dense but accessible read for most parents, and is definitely recommended for therapists working with older adopted children. Richard Rose's book *Life Story Therapy With Traumatized Children* gives a clear and structured outline for using life stories with children. It's forward by Bruce Perry makes it clear that everyone has a right to their story—and the devastating impact of being without one.

19. Again, the works of Dan Hughes are very helpful here. Also helpful to parents and children are the very readable books of

Brenda McCreight, including *Parenting Your Older Adopted Child*, for parents, and *Help I've Been Adopted* For teens and older children.

20. Again, the work of Diane Malbin has been useful here. A very good book on Sensory Integration Disorder is Lucy Miller and Doris Fuller's *Sensational Kids: Hope and Help for children with Sensory Processing Disorder.*

21. Deborah Rutman and her colleagues at University of Victoria in BC have recently completed a 3-year longitudinal study of children who age out in foster care. See Works Cited.

22. According to Roderic Beaujot at the University of Western Ontario, 41% of Canadians between 20 and 29 years of age lived with their parents in 2001.

23. The Attachment Association of Canada maintains a list of therapists who are trained to work with children and families who are experiencing challenges in attachment. Their website is at www. attachmentcan.ca.

Works Cited

Beaujot, Roderic. *Delayed Life Transitions: Trends and Implications.* Vanier Institute, 2004. Accessed online at http://www.vanierinstitute. ca

Briere, John. *Principles of Trauma Therapy: A guide to symptoms, evaluation and treatment, 2nd Edition.* Los Angeles: Sage Publications, 2013

CanFASD Website: www.canfasd.ca

Densmore, Robert. *FASD Relationships.* Salmon Arm, BC: Dory Spirit Books Ltd., 2011.

Erikson, Erik. *Childhood and Society.* New York: Norton, 1963.

Erikson, Erik. The Life Cycle Completed: a review. New York: Norton, 1982.

DeLoache, Judy S. and Brown, Ann L. Looking for Big Bird: Studies of Memory in Very Young Children. *Quarterly Newlsletter of the Laboratory of Comparative Human Cognition, Volume 1, Number 3,* p. 53-57, 1979.

Haycock, Phillip. Fetal Alcohol Spectrum Disorders: the Epigenetic Perspective. *Biology of Reproduction, 81(4)* 607-617. Accessed online at http://www.biolreprod.org/content/81/4/607.full. 2013.

Hickling, Meg. *Boys, Girls and Body Science: a first book about the facts of life*, Madeira Park, BC: Harbour Publishing, 2002.

Hickling, Meg. *The New Speaking of Sex: What your children need to know and when they need to know it*, Kelowna, BC: Northstone Publishing, 2005.

Hughes, Daniel. *Building the Bonds of Attachment: awakening love in deeply troubled children, 2nd ed.* Lanham, Maryland: Jason Aronson, 2006.

Hughes, Daniel. *Attachment-Focused Parenting: effective strategies to care for children.* New York: Norton & Co, 2009.

John Howard Society of Ontario. *Fetal Alcohol Spectrum Disorder and the Criminal Justice System: A poor fit.* Fact Sheet 26, 2010. Accessed online at http://johnhoward.on.ca/pdfs/FactSheet_26_FASD_and_the_Criminal_Justice_System.pdf

Lange, S. Shield, K., Rehm, J., Popova, S. Prevalence of fetal alcohol spectrum disorders in child care settings: a meta-analysis. *Pediatrics,* 2013 Oct;132(4), accessed through PubMed at http://www.ncbi.nlm.nih.gov/pubmed/24019412

Malbin, Diana. *Fetal Alcohol Specturm Disorders: Trying Differently Rather than Harder.* Portland, Oregon: FASCETS, Inc., 2002.

McCreight, Brenda. *Parenting Your Older Adopted Child.* Oakland, CA: New Harbinger Press, 2002.

McCreight, Brenda. *Help I've Been Adopted.* Milford, CT: Adoption Ed, LLC, 2010.

Miller, Lucy J. and Fuller, Doris A. *Sensational Kids: Hope and Help for Children with Sensory Processing Disorder.* Berkley:Peregee Trade: 2007.

Neufeld, Gordon. *The Vital Connection*, DVD available from website www.gordonneufeld.com/products, 2010.

Perry, Bruce. Child Trauma Academy website: http://www.childtrauma.org.

Perry, Bruce. *The Boy Who Was Raised as a Dog and other stories from a Child Psychiatrist's Notebook.* New York: Basic Books, 2006.

Perry, Bruce. *Born for Love.* New York: Harper Collins, 2010.

Rose, Richard. *Life Story Therapy with Traumatized Children.* Philidelphia, PA: Jessica Kingsley Publishers, 2012.

Rutman, Deborah, Hubberstey, Carol, and Feduniw, April. When You Age Out of Care—Where to From There? Research Initiatives for Social Change Unit, School of Social Work, University of Victoria, Victoria, BC. Available online at http://www.uvic.ca/hsd/socialwork/assets/docs/research/WhenYouthAge2007.pdf

Siegel, Daniel. *The Whole-Brain Child: 12 revolutionary strategies to nurture your child's developing mind.* New York: Delacorte Press, 2011.

Smith, Monique Gray. *Tilly: A Story of Hope and Reilience.* Winlaw, BC: Sononis Press, 2013.

Truth and Reconcilliation Commission or Canada. Truth and Reconcilliation Canada Website: www.trc.ca

Weinberg, J., Sliwowska, J.G., Hellemans, K.G.C. Prenatal alcohol exposure: Foetal programming, the hypothalamic-pituitary-adrenal axis and sex differences in outcome. J. *Neuroendo.* 20:470-488, 2008.

About the Authors

Dr. Serena Patterson, who wrote *Faith, Hunter and the Ancestors: An Adoption Story* is a clinical psychologist who has over 25 years experience in working with and teaching about children and families. Her lifelong passion for children whose first families could not raise them to adulthood began in 1982, when she spent a volunteer year at Buckhorn Children's Center in Buckhorn, Kentucky. Inspired by the courage and the obstacles of the Buckhorn children, she completed her Ph.D. in Clinical Psychology at Simon Fraser University in Burnaby, BC, in 1992.

Monika Grünberg is a Clinical Counsellor who has worked with families and children for 20 years. Ms. Grünberg grew up in Germany, a country that has worked very hard to tell the difficult truths and heal the scars of extreme prejudice and war. She came to Canada in 1981, and studied Anthropology and Psychology before completing her Masters Degree in Counselling at the University of British Columbia.

Dr. Patterson and Ms. Grünberg are partners in life, in writing and in private practice. They have parented three children: one biological, one fostered, and one adopted. More of their writing can be found on their website: www.grunbergpatterson.ca

There you can also find out about their therapy services, upcoming events, and products for adoptive families.

About the Illustrator

Scottish-born Claire Kjundzic is a graphic designer, illustator, print-maker, sculter and painter. Her work has been widely reproduced by groups including the International Congress of Midwives, Amnesty International and Oxfam, and was featured in the athletes' living rooms at the 2010 Olympics in Vancouver.

Acknowledgements

The authors wish to thank Occupational Therapist and gifted teacher Kim Barthel for her encouragement of this manuscript and for the many things that we have learned from her about attachment, sensory processing, addictions, and more. Kee Warner and the people at White Crow Village have been invaluable over the last three years as consultants and support to our family. Dr. Ulrika Sunder-Harding, Dr. Brenda Knight, and Dr Candance Orcutt were therapists to the therapists, helping us hold together through challenges we never even imagined until adoption changed our lives. Cathie Gilbert, our support worker through the BC Adoptive Families Association, has a wealth of knowledge and experience, and a seemingly endless supply of hope and of faith in the resiliance of children, and of parents. Monika's mother, Waltraut Grünberg, helped with the details to make Oma Mika's story believable. Serena's father, Rev. John Patterson, died before this work began but seemed to whisper his lines into her ear as the friendly, slightly pompous ghost of Grandpa Green. Our beloved fur-children, Molly and Frost, are the models for both the character and the drawings of Roscoe. We would be lost without their daily gift of unconditional, joyful love in our house. Each of our children con- tributed insights and encouragement to the story. Many others have contributed to the ideas here; some have published works that we've cited, others have given us friendship. All are treasured.

CPSIA information can be obtained at www.ICGtesting.com
Printed in the USA
LVOW06s0514090714

393247LV00001BA/1/P